CONVERSATIONS WITH THE MONK

JONATHAN FANNING

CONVERSATIONS WITH THE MONK

FIRST EDITION

ISBN
979-832300888-9

For more information on this title and other books, videos, audio clips with "the Monk", keynotes, retreats, pilgrimages and speaking engagements, please visit us online:

www.JonathanFanning.com

Printed in the United States of America.

Contents

1. What would You Ask?

You are stranded for several days in a cabin, deep in the woods, with no electricity, no books, no games, no internet connection, no phones, no electronics whatsoever. You have plenty of food, a warm fire, a seemingly endless supply of seasoned firewood, and an old-fashioned – but fully functional – wood stove. You are alone with your thoughts and the Monk. Yes, the Monk. The two of you will wait out an incredible winter storm together. The Monk is a gifted chef. In fact, he seems to be very gifted at just about everything. He is well-read in every topic you bring up. His memory is sharp and his gift for story-telling unsurpassed. The Monk understands and has thought deeply on all of life's questions. Any question you offer is handled masterfully, from multiple angles and perspectives. The Monk welcomes dialogue with a deep and heartfelt kindness that perfectly complements the fire's warm glow.

When I first met *the Monk* who inspired this book, I had a lot of questions… questions about faith, purpose, rules, meaning, money, parenting, authority, laws, history, truth, judgement… Sharing a meal with the Monk was like breaking bread with Mother Teresa, Saint Francis, Catherine of Siena, Aquinas and Einstein. Brother was wise, passionate and real. He loved hearing your questions and stories. And people came from far and wide to hear his questions and stories. After every interaction, I left both comforted and challenged. As the Monk often said, "People go where they're fed. 2,000 years ago and today." He fed people. Physically, emotionally, intellectually and spiritually. And people came back for more.

Are you on a quest to find answers? Are you ready to wrestle with some of life's most important questions? If so, bring your questions. Let's pursue what's true and good and beautiful together. The following pages are but a small sampling of conversations with the Monk.

www.JonathanFanning.com/monk

2. I'm Spiritual, not Religious

Thomas: What's wrong with being spiritual? Isn't religion just a crutch?

Monk: Nothing and yes.

Thomas: Really?

Monk: Yes.

Thomas: I'm serious.

Monk: So am I.

Thomas: I can't believe that you, a hardcore religious fanatic, would say…

Monk: Ha!!! Me, a hardcore religious fanatic?

Thomas: You are a monk, aren't you?

Monk: That I am. Guilty, as charged.

Thomas: Aren't monks about as religious as you can get?

Monk: What do you mean by religious?

Thomas: All the stuff. The rules, the ceremonies, rigid beliefs, ancient old-fashioned traditions. Things you have to do. Things you have to say. All that stuff!

Monk: Ancient. Thank you, Thomas! Look at me, do I have a lot of stuff?

Thomas: Funny, Brother. You do have a lot of candles and religious books. And robes. You definitely have a lot of old-fashioned customs.

Monk: Shall we go back to your question?

Thomas: Please do. I hear it all the time… "I'm spiritual, not religious." Sometimes people even say it in that condescending tone that religious people are famous for!

Monk: Is that so? Have these "spiritual but not religious" believers adopted the snobbish attitude of the "religious but not spiritual"?

Thomas: Oh, that's good. Who are you picking on?

Monk: No one in particular. And human nature in all of us! Thomas, what is your real question?

Thomas: My real question? Isn't religion a crutch? Is it truly necessary?

Monk: You do enjoy asking multiple questions! Let's have an honest look at them. A crutch? Absolutely. You didn't realize that you are a cripple in need of a crutch?

Thomas: How so?

Monk: Tell me, Thomas, how is your relationship with your God and His creation?

Thomas: It's… wait! We're not talking about me here. I'm asking about the people who say they're spiritual but not religious.

Monk: Should I give you some time to wrestle with the question? Surely you don't think the Questioner will let you pass on that question forever! The people you speak of: how is their relationship with God and His creation?

Thomas: Good?

Monk: Good? Are you sure?

Thomas: Far from perfect. If we're trying to be honest here, you could say that about all of us.

Monk: He speaks the truth! I like that "trying to be honest." Shouldn't that always be the intent?

Thomas: Right. The relationship is okay for some. Who has the perfect relationship with the creator and creation?

Monk: That's the point. We're all cripples when it comes to relationship to God. We demonstrate it in the way we treat his children. That's why we need a crutch. You asked if religion is necessary. Is it?

Thomas: I thought I was asking the questions and you were answering them!

Monk: We're both looking for answers, Thomas. I've only met one who has all the answers. And even He liked to ask questions.

Thomas: You're too much.

Monk: I'll take that as a compliment! Is religion necessary?

Thomas: I'm not convinced that it is.

Monk: That's fair. And honest. Good. We're making progress.

Thomas: We are?

Monk: Certainly. Seek and you shall find. What does that mean?

Thomas: Again, you're asking me? I think it means you find what you're looking for. Isn't it rather self-explanatory?

Monk: Seek the Truth and you shall find the Truth.

Thomas: Oh. That's better than my answer.

Monk: His answers are always pretty good!

Thomas: Convince me that I need religion.

Monk: And why would I do that?

Thomas: Isn't that your job?

Monk: Not at all.

Thomas: I'm confused then. I thought that you religious people were supposed to convince other people that they need religion.

Monk: Thomas, do you like to travel?

Thomas: Absolutely.

Monk: Where?

Thomas: Just about anywhere. Around the US. Europe.

Monk: Have you visited my native country, Italy?

Thomas: Yes, I have! What a country!

Monk: How do you get there from here?

Thomas: Fly. What do you mean?

Monk: Fly. Yes. From where to where?

Thomas: I'd fly from New York to Rome.

Monk: Okay. When you get to Italy, how do you get around?

Thomas: I rent a car. You can take the train. Some tourists take the bus. Some never leave Rome. But I like to see the places that are off the beaten path.

Monk: That's my kind of traveling! So you *need* a plane and you *need* a car to see Italy?

Thomas: Well, no. You don't *need* a car. I guess you don't *need* the plane either. You could get there by boat and, like I said, there are a lot of ways to get around once you're in Italy.

Monk: You need some form of transportation?

Thomas: Yes… Is this a trick question? You could swim, but I don't think any human being could really swim the Atlantic.

Monk: Hmmm.

Thomas: Hmmm what?

Monk: Hmmm.

Thomas: Ok. You're saying people *need* religion like they need a boat or plane. But what if I can get there without it?

Monk: Can you?

Thomas: Again, aren't you supposed to help me answer my questions?

Monk: Do you need me to get closer to the truth, much like you need a mode of transportation to get closer to seeing Italy?

Thomas: No. I'm not buying it.

Monk: I'm not asking you to buy anything. You asked the question. Really, you asked a whole series of questions. Do you really want to find answers?

Thomas: Of course I want to find answers.

Monk: Not "of course." Plenty of people say they want to find answers, yet their actions demonstrate that they don't.

Thomas: You think so?

Monk: I don't just think so. I know so. I'm very guilty of this. I've asked plenty of questions when I don't want to find an answer. Or when I've already decided what I'm going to do and my question is just designed to support the decision I've already made.

Thomas: For example?

Monk: Someone gives me feedback that I don't like. I ask, "Why are you telling me this?" But I've already decided that they're giving me the feedback because they want something or because they don't know the whole situation. They answer my question, "I think it's something you need to hear." And I assume that there's still something more to the feedback. Or I'll ask "Why does this keep happening to me?" although I've already decided that there's nothing I can do to change my circumstances. Do I really want to know why this keeps happening to me? Do I really want an answer to my question? No.

Thomas: That hits close to home. You're not perfect, either?

Monk: Oh, far from it! Saint John of the Cross spoke about a pane of glass. When the glass is held up to the light, we see all of its imperfections. We avoid holding the glass up to the light because we don't want to see the imperfections.

Thomas: Does this answer my question?

Monk: What kind of answer do you want?

Thomas: I want to know.

Monk: Religion is a vehicle to help get us to the right relationship with God and His creation. Can we get there without religion? Can you get to Italy without a map?

Thomas: Yes.

Monk: Yes. If you've never been to Italy, how likely would you be to make it to Florence without a map?

Thomas: I might stop and ask for directions.

Monk: That's where all the "stuff" of religion came from. People who found a path towards building a tremendous relationship with God left a map.

Thomas: But I can get there without the map.

Monk: Maybe. You can also waste a lot of time and energy. Or drown in the Atlantic. Not all paths are the same. We recognize this in every other area of life, from fitness to business to saving for retirement. For some reason, we have a stubborn streak when it comes to finding God.

Thomas: Is this a modern phenomenon?

Monk: Not at all! Have you ever heard of the Old Testament?

Thomas: Very funny.

Monk: The Old Testament is story after story of people that don't want the map. They don't need the map. They're on the beaches of Long Island and about to swim a few thousand miles. They don't need a map. They don't need a boat. They don't even want flippers. God reaches out to them over and over again, saying, "Come, follow me. Here's the map. Here's the way. You want a deeper joy – a lasting happiness – that you know exists but seems ever elusive. Follow me. You're cripple. Here's a crutch."

Thomas: So then your answer is yes, we need religion?

Monk: Show me a person in the right relationship with their God and His creation and I'll show you a person who knows how desperately we all need a map!

Thomas: So many explorers didn't have maps.

Monk: And then they made maps. If they wanted to make the trip again or help others make the trip, they made very detailed maps. The maps said "go here" – "stay away from there!" The maps were full of lessons and warnings. Even Ben Franklin was charting the tides on his trips across the Atlantic to get a better idea of the best timing for the journey.

Thomas: I'll have to think about this.

Monk: No. You don't have to think about it. One of our greatest gifts is the ability to choose what we think about. Here's a question for you: Is it worth thinking about?

Thomas: Yes.

3. Most Important Questions?

Thomas: Looks like we'll be stuck here for a while.
Monk: Stuck?
Thomas: Yes, stuck. The weather isn't letting up. If anything, the snow is getting more intense. We're not going anywhere.
Monk: And that's a bad thing?
Thomas: Yeah.
Monk: What makes it a bad thing?
Thomas: Being stuck is always a bad thing. How could it not be a bad thing?
Monk: Are you sure? Could it be that you're ignoring two of life's most important questions?
Thomas: What? Are you referring to the difference between good and bad?
Monk: No. Something more basic. Maybe easier to ignore.
Thomas: Okay, I'll bite. What are your two questions?
Monk: Well, they're certainly not my questions. They're yours, as well. These two questions affect every aspect of our lives.
Thomas: Of course they do. Please do fill me in!
Monk: What do you believe and why do you believe it?
Thomas: Faith questions?
Monk: Not specifically, although they most certainly deal with faith, as well. What do you believe about money, success, family, relationships, weather, faith, what's bad or good, and yes, even about being *stuck*!
Thomas: Ah, philosophy! Don't you think most people would agree that being stuck in a snow storm talking about philosophy is a bad thing? [they both laugh] I suppose your two questions are important, but don't most questions have that same importance?
Monk: You're joking, right?
Thomas: No.
Monk: William James once said that most questions philosophers

fool around with aren't worth the time because *they made no difference*. Do all questions make the same difference? Do these two questions make a difference? Do you invest enough time on questions that make a difference?

Thomas: You make a good point.

Monk: Well, thank you. Do you have an answer?

Thomas: All questions do not make the same difference. For example, "Do you like the snow?" makes a difference, but certainly not as much of a difference as "Do we have enough wood to keep ourselves warm throughout this storm?" Some questions affect life itself. Some affect many lives. Many questions affect how we spend our lives. From that perspective, your first question makes a big difference. What do you believe about time, education, work/life balance, parenting, the role of government, living a so-called good life. You know, Brother, you might be on to something. How about this one: "What do you believe about the meaning of life?" That's a question that makes a difference.

Monk: Is it?

Thomas: That's a massive question. But unanswerable.

Monk: Unanswerable? Are you sure?

Thomas: Hmm. I think so.

Monk: Let's come back to that. Under William James' criteria, you are sure that it's a question that makes a difference?

Thomas: Oh yeah! I'm sure of that.

Monk: Then it's worth spending time on? [Chuckles] Thomas, my deepest apologies for ending that sentence with a preposition. If memory serves, Winston Churchill, the great linguist, was fond of saying, "Ending a sentence with a preposition is something up with which I will not put."

Thomas: You and your quotes… you never cease to amaze!

Monk: Flattery won't get you out of answering the question.

Thomas: Yes. It's a question… on which it is worth spending time.

Monk: Good. And have you? Will you?

Thomas: I haven't, at least not much. Will I? That depends.
Monk: Why would it depend?
Thomas: It depends on the possibility of finding an answer.
Monk: That's not true.
Thomas: How can you say that? It most certainly is true. Who knows the answer?
Monk: I would suggest that you already operate from an answer to the question, "What do I believe about the meaning of life?"
Thomas: Please enlighten me.
Monk: Enlighten. To shed light on. Light is good, if you want to see and be seen.
Thomas: You're too much!
Monk: Thank you, Thomas. So are you. And I expect that will make "being stuck" here much more bearable. Perhaps even enjoyable!
Thomas: We'll see.
Monk: Light. Socrates wisely said "The unexamined life is not worth living." We could paraphrase him in so many areas. The unexamined leader is not worth following. The unexamined business is not worth investing in. The unexamined teacher is not worth learning from. There I go again – ending with prepositions!
Thomas: Thanks for the language lesson! You're suggesting that I examine, shed light on, what I believe about the meaning of life. I suppose the simplest starting point would be something you've just made more clear to me. I believe it's an unanswerable question. How's that for clarity?
Monk: To see and to be seen! Now that we see this, what's next?
Thomas: With your light metaphor, I can see that my actions demonstrate some of what I believe about the question. The ideas I'm thinking about are vague, but bear with me. The meaning of life – or what I believe about it – includes not wasting life, doing something good, spending time with family and friends, becoming successful.
Monk: And you believe that you're supposed to do all these things?

Or pursue all these things?

Thomas: I suppose my answer is yes.

Monk: Is there more to it?

Thomas: Probably. To your point, I don't think I've given the question adequate time.

Monk: Would you say that's likely true for most people?

Thomas: I would. It's comforting to know that I'm not alone! But, if it's such an important question, how do so many people practically ignore it?

Monk: Do they know that the question exists?

Thomas: Sure.

Monk: Do they know that it's extremely important?

Thomas: I think that answer would also be yes.

Monk: Then it's part of the know-do gap. There's often a massive gap between what we know and what we do. We know a lot about saving for retirement, healthy living, being a good spouse… We don't always do what we know!

Thomas: You could be a business consultant or some kind of life-coach. A man of many talents!

Monk: Very funny. I don't need another job, but the truth does apply to every aspect of life. Do you believe that it's possible to know more about the meaning or purpose of life?

Thomas: I'm not sure.

Monk: That's light! To see and be seen. Excellent.

Thomas: Why is it excellent to be unsure? Wouldn't it be better to have an answer?

Monk: Would you prefer to find answers to less important questions or to realize that you don't yet have answers to some of the most important questions?

Thomas: You make a valid point.

Monk: From your earlier answers – don't waste life, do something good, yada yada yada – Thomas, am I right in assuming you do think that at least some aspect of the meaning of life can be known?

Thomas: I'll go with yes. Well, at least for my life.
Monk: Ok. And is there a commonality, some overlap, between the purpose of your life and the purpose of others' lives?
Thomas: I think there would be, but I'm not so sure how much of a commonality.
Monk: I've always enjoyed W.H. Auden's quip: "We are all here on earth to help others; what on earth the others are here for, I don't know." If we just look at one of your beliefs, is it true for everybody that we are not to *waste life*?
Thomas: No one should waste life, but from there it gets sticky. How would we define wasting life? Is eating ice cream a waste of life? Taking an afternoon nap? Working overtime to help put your kids through college? Reading for pleasure? Buying flowers?
Monk: Thomas! Wasn't that phrase, don't waste life, your phrase?
Thomas: Yes, it was. I guess *I* need to have a definition. Maybe it's as simple as spending time on important things.
Monk: Important to whom?
Thomas: To me. And to people I care about. No, it's more than that. Important in relation to life, community, the world around me.
Monk: Like the famous Teddy Roosevelt line, "spend yourself in a worthy cause!"
Thomas: Absolutely. When you phrase it that way, I do believe it just might be something we all have in common.
Monk: Is it more than that?
Thomas: Perhaps, but can we just stay with that for the moment?
Monk: Sure. Spend yourself. In a worthy cause. Two components. What does it mean to spend yourself?
Thomas: Give what you've got.
Monk: All of it?
Thomas: No. Not necessarily all.
Monk: Most?
Thomas: Oh boy. I thought we were close.
Monk: And now we're not?

Thomas: Well, you keep asking questions.
Monk: Of course I do. We're on a quest. What's the root of the word question?
Thomas: Quest.
Monk: And you and I, together, are on a quest. We're looking for the answer, or answers. Questions are a tool to help us with our quest. Naturally, like any tools, questions can be used for many purposes, even to achieve the opposite of their intended purpose.
Thomas: The opposite?
Monk: Certainly. A hammer can be used to build or destroy. Medicine can be used to heal or to kill. Food can be used in a healthy and nourishing way or not. Influence can be used to encourage or discourage. The Greeks used the word, "Telos." Aristotle would describe a good clock as a clock that fulfilled its telos or purpose of keeping time. A question that fulfills its telos helps guide the quest.
Thomas: And what's the purpose, or telos, of the quest?
Monk: A quest can have many purposes, but in our context, I believe that we are hoping to arrive at an answer. A true answer. A "what is" answer.
Thomas: What do you mean by a "what is" answer?
Monk: It's simply another way of saying truth. Of saying that we want to shed light on what is really there.
Thomas: Of what I really believe?
Monk: And why you really believe it.
Thomas: I forgot that part. Is that second question as important as the first?
Monk: Doesn't it hold up the first?
Thomas: Meaning?
Monk: From your own career, would you say that you believe starting a business is risky? And why? Why do you believe what you believe about starting a business?
Thomas: Starting a business may seem risky, but I do not believe that it is. Why? Because you have control over so much of the

process. You can start small. You get to decide what to sell, where to sell it, what to charge, who to hire.

Monk: Why do you believe this?

Thomas: Didn't I just explain that?

Monk: Not entirely. Why do you believe those reasons are "what is" – in other words, true?

Thomas: Oh. From experience. Mine and others. Since I hear so many people say that it's risky to start a business, I've also spent considerable time thinking through the question, "Is it risky to start a business?"

Monk: Aha! You've invested time to figure out what you believe and why you believe it.

Thomas: Sure I have. Because it matters.

Monk: Right. The "Why" matters because we need a real reason to believe the things we believe. Why did it matter a lot to you?

Thomas: That's easy. I wanted to start a business. In the process of investing a massive amount of time, energy, money, and emotion into starting a business, it was very important to know what I believed and why.

Monk: It was an extremely logical investment of thought time!

Thomas: Thank you, Brother!

Monk: Can I ask you a question that might be a bit uncomfortable?

Thomas: Go ahead.

Monk: Are there more important beliefs that you have not been willing to put under the same spotlight?

Thomas: For example?

Monk: What do you believe and why do you believe it in regards to a higher power, a creator, a "God"?

Thomas: Ummm. You got me there. But I have spent some time thinking about it.

Monk: Some?

Thomas: Yeah, some. I guess work, life, all of that stuff was maybe more important.

Monk: I see.
Thomas: You do?
Monk: Yes. Do you?
Thomas: Do I what?
Monk: Do you see?
Thomas: I think so, but what are you getting at?
Monk: What is the telos of the question, the purpose of the quest? Isn't it the same as before? To find out what is.
Thomas: You're saying that what I believe about a higher power isn't that important to me?
Monk: No. You said that. I didn't have to. We just shed light on your actions, the way you prioritize time. Once the light was on, we saw the truth. You haven't treated that question as an important one.
Thomas: Do I have to?
Monk: Come on, Thomas! You know the answer to that. That's like asking, "Do I have to change the oil in my car?" No. But the car certainly won't come close to fulfilling its telos without proper care and attention.
Thomas: Okay, but oil is only one of many things a car needs.
Monk: Right. And knowing how and why you came to exist and for what purpose is only one of many questions you need to answer! Is there a God or is there not? Before we get to that question, let's look at another. How important is the answer? Does the question matter? Does it make a difference in your life whether there is a God or not? Let me paraphrase C.S. Lewis with a good deal of poetic license: If God exists, that is of infinite importance. If God does not exist, that is of no importance. The only thing the existence of God cannot be is moderately important.
Thomas: Here goes the monk, trying to convert me! Leaping from harmless questions like what do I believe about business to the deadly question, what do I believe about God?
Monk: Thomas, Thomas, Thomas! Only shedding light. Only pursuing some of life's most important questions. Our arrival at this

question of the existence of a creator is unavoidable.

Thomas: Unavoidable? How so? Maybe because you were going to take the conversation there whether I were a willing participant or not!

Monk: Unavoidable for a very different and very fundamental reason. The leaning tower of Pisa leans at the top, does it not?

Thomas: The whole things leans. What do you mean, at the top?

Monk: I mean the top is out of alignment from the bottom.

Thomas: I think so. I remember a big construction project to keep it from falling over, but I don't think they got rid of the lean. They needed to maintain the lean or it would become the plain old tower of Pisa!

Monk: That's right. The project was particularly difficult because the goal was to keep the tower crooked but not allow it to fall over.

Thomas: And? Where are you going? What's your telos, Brother?

Monk: If you are building a tower of any significance, the first few layers of stones, the layers upon which the entire weight of the structure rests, how important is it that they be sound or "true"?

Thomas: Very.

Monk: What you believe about the meaning of life… would this "stone" go under or above the "stone" that asks whether or not a creator exists?

Thomas: We can skip that layer. We don't know the answer. No one does.

Monk: And why do you believe that?

Thomas: Enough of the what do you believe and why do you believe it!

Monk: Are you sure? Is the light uncomfortable or is it what the light allows you to see?

Thomas: People don't have to deal with the creator question.

Monk: More progress! You ever buy tires for your car?

Thomas: Of course.

Monk: What tires?

Thomas: I don't know. Why?
Monk: Do you look at the telos of the tires before you buy them?
Thomas: Certainly. You're talking about snow tires versus all season, right? And the speed ratings?
Monk: You build your decision on the creator's purpose, more commonly known in the tire world as the manufacturer's specs. Was that tire designed and built for speed? Long life? Fuel efficiency? Snow? Rain? Road noise? Your tires were designed and manufactured with a telos, with a purpose, with an end in mind.
Thomas: Okay, I'll play along. But what if there is no creator? Or what if that creator just created the raw ingredients for life and allowed it to go from there? What if that creator had no purpose, no end, in mind? What if the telos was just for the creator's entertainment… let's see what they do!
Monk: Hold on! I love the enthusiasm and the questions. Why don't we revisit some of those later on? I think your questions are worthy of our quest. Allow me to flip them around. What if there is a creator and that creator had a very specific purpose for creating you? Would that question affect the next "stone" on our tower?
Thomas: Yes, it absolutely would.
Monk: Should we take a look? You see why I called it unavoidable? Throughout history, most of mankind has found this question unavoidable.
Thomas: Unavoidable, perhaps. But it's also unanswerable.
Monk: Is that what you believe? Why do you believe that?
Thomas: You and your questions!
Monk: Here's a line of thinking that I believe is unavoidable if we are honest in our quest. A ladder is a good ladder if it does what it was designed to do. A fitness routine is a good fitness routine if it does what it was designed to do. Fulfilling a purpose is related to the purpose intended by the designer. If you and I have a designer, then that designer had some purpose in mind. If we lay the stone of "why am I here?" before laying the stone of "is there a creator?",

don't we run a significant risk of placing that second stone on quicksand?

Thomas: I don't know. I'm not seeing a good argument against what you just said, but…

Monk: But what, Thomas?

Thomas: Can we know if there is a creator or not? Even if we could, how can we know if that creator had any purpose in mind when creating us?

Monk: These are excellent questions, worthy of pursuit. Do you ask the questions because you intend to seek answers or as a means to avoid seeking answers?

Thomas: Ouch!

Monk: Thomas, let's try approaching this question from a familiar angle. What do you believe about education?

Thomas: Education? Well, it's important. It will affect career options. It can open doors. It's valuable, but need not necessarily be formal education. School and education are not synonymous. One can attend a lot of school without gaining much education. The opposite is also true. Lincoln was largely self-educated. I've learned more from books outside of school than I have during school. The…

Monk: Okay! Okay! You have a lot of beliefs about education. Try this: can you summarize clearly and simply the "Why" you believe what you believe about education?

Thomas: Clear and simple… that's a challenge…. Experience. Mine and others.

Monk: So you learned from life and, as Isaac Newton said about his accomplishments: you stood on the shoulders of giants.

Thomas: That's accurate.

Monk: Why don't we do this: I'm getting hungry. We have a cupboard full of food. I'll dig through there to see what I can make us for lunch. Can you bring some wood in from the front porch and get that old wood stove cranking? We can talk more over lunch.

Thomas: I like the plan.

4. God Exists? Prove it!

Monk: Where were we?

Thomas: Does a creator exist or not? Can we know? If we could know – and did know our creator's intentions – we would have significant clues about our big question, "What is the meaning of life?" It's worth our time because, as one of the 50 or so people you quoted liked to say, spend time on questions that make a difference.

Monk: Excellent summary, Thomas. If I recall, you also mentioned that we can learn from our own experiences or the experiences of others. How did you learn to walk?

Thomas: Both of those approaches. I had people around me who knew how to walk. They demonstrated and I observed.

Monk: Can we know that a Creator exists?

Thomas: No.

Monk: That settles it. Conversation over.

Thomas: You're giving up that easily?

Monk: Am I? Or are you?

Thomas: Touché!

Monk: Have you ever read Plato's cave allegory?

Thomas: Probably in college, but I would need a refresher. Is it relevant?

Monk: Let me give you the monk's extremely abbreviated, overly simplified, and slightly modified version. You're stuck in a cave with no light. Do you need someone to carry you out of the cave or just hand you a light and a good map?

Thomas: I'd say that the light and map would suffice.

Monk: Excellent answer. When I asked if you were giving up that easily, I was merely handing you a light and map. What you saw, unless you chose to look away or extinguish the light, was that you are not stuck in the cave. You have the tools to work your way out, but you get to choose whether or not to use those tools.

Thomas: Why are you smiling at me?

Monk: Because I once was lost, as well. And I didn't want to be found. You could have handed me a light or even showed me an illuminated path that led straight out of the cave. I would have turned you down. Thomas, I want you to think about this. There are answers to your questions. You may not find, understand, agree with or like all the answers in this lifetime; but there are answers to your questions. We quite often resist most what we need most.

Thomas: I find that idea both refreshing and daunting. It would seem the responsibility is on me.

Monk: It is and it's not. Take up your cross and follow me. My yoke is easy and my burden light. Simon and Garfunkel had that mysteriously wonderful line, "Like a bridge over troubled waters, I will lay me down." Thomas, we've been promised help.

Thomas: It sounds too good to be true.

Monk: It's too good to be made up!

Thomas: Go back to the cave scenario. Plato, right?

Monk: Yes. Plato's cave is about seeing what is. Shedding the scales from our eyes. Seeing what's real, not just a dim reflection.

Thomas: What if no one comes along with a light? What if a person never gets stuck in a cabin with a monk to provide enlightenment?

Monk: Hmmm. Another one of the world's most brilliant minds, Blaise Pascal. You surely remember him from mathematics. We use Pascal's Law every day when we step on the brakes in a car. The brake fluid pressure is transferred through the braking system.

Thomas: A monk teaching physics!

Monk: Why do you laugh?

Thomas: I'm sorry, but it just seems funny. Religion and science, together at last.

Monk: Oh, Thomas, you don't know your history, do you? Religion has been responsible for more scientific advancement than your culture cares to admit. Isaac Newton wrote more about God than mathematics. He was convinced that the infinite creator must have designed the world in such a way that its governing laws could be discovered and harnessed by us, creatures made in his image.

Thomas: Are you sure?

Monk: Quite! Can we get back to Pascal now, and a question that makes a tremendous difference?

Thomas: Okay, but if we're stuck in this cabin long enough, I'm coming back to this religion and science topic. I'm quite certain that religion has to answer for some terrible things.

Monk: Pascal spent a lot of time wrestling with important questions. He once wrote there is enough light for those who want to find God and enough shadows so that you don't have to find God if you don't want to. Pascal went on to say that there are 3 types of people in the world: those who seek God and have found Him, those who seek God and will find Him, and those who neither seek God nor want to find Him.

Thomas: Wouldn't everyone want to find God, if God exists?

Monk: Absolutely not!

Thomas: You say that with a profound conviction. I'm not so sure.

Monk: Even many people who are quite convinced that God exists try to avoid him. Why? It's glaringly obvious. The God who is, the True God, makes us uncomfortable.

Thomas: Uncomfortable?

Monk: Oh yeah! Extremely.

Thomas: How so?

Monk: In just about every way imaginable. You ever play sports?

Thomas: Sure. Plenty.

Monk: Were all of your coaches good?

Thomas: Oh no. But I did have a few very good coaches.

Monk: The best coaches, did they make you uncomfortable?

Thomas: Constantly. I see what you're saying. The best coaches challenge us to pursue our potential, individually and as a team.

Monk: Did the best coaches allow you to play selfishly? Did they encourage you to do whatever you felt like in the moment?

Thomas: Not at all. They knew what was best for us, sometimes even when we didn't understand that. I had a basketball coach who ran us more the day after holiday weekends or Christmas break than any other day. He even raised the temperature in our gym for practices. He constantly reiterated that we would be the best conditioned team in the league and that we would have more energy left in the 4th quarter or overtime than any of our opponents. He said that would make the difference in some big games.

Monk: Was he right?

Thomas: It made all the difference in several playoff games that season. But I don't think we believed him or liked his process until we were cutting down the nets at the end of the season as league champions!

Monk: That's exactly why some don't look for God. It's the same reason a child might avoid mom or dad when they know they've not lived up to a promise. We've all been there: "Finish your homework before you go out to play with your friends."

Thomas: Makes sense. But is God like that?

Monk: C.S. Lewis said we want not so much a Father in Heaven as a Grandfather in Heaven. Most religions have been consistent in describing God as a Father. Augustine of Hippo said we love the truth when it enlightens us but hate the truth when it convicts us.

Thomas: I like that. The grandfather might let you get away with eating M&M's for breakfast!

Monk: Back to Pascal… his famous proposal is known as Pascal's Wager. Pascal gives us 4 options. [Drawing on a scrap of paper as he speaks]

	We believe	We do not believe
God exists		
God does not exist		

Thomas: Aren't there more options?

Monk: Sure. There are nuances, as our confused culture likes to point out.

Thomas: Why do you say confused culture?
Monk: Should I say intentionally confused? It hinges on the telos. Are we introducing complexity, or nuances, because it helps in the search for truth or because we want an excuse to avoid the truth? The human heart has an incredible capacity for justification!
Thomas: Bear with me. I'm thinking of the nuances. For example, what kind of a God do we believe in? One god or many? A personal god or an indifferent god?
Monk: The options fit in Pascal's Wager. Look through the grid. What do you stand to lose if you're wrong in each situation? Some of us have more faith in doubt than we do in blatantly obvious evidence.
Thomas: Blatantly obvious? Give me an example.
Monk: I'll give you several. But first, will you answer this in respect to Pascal's 3 types of people: do you want to find out if a creator exists?
Thomas: I think so. What did you mean by faith in doubt?
Monk: Many people have an almost arrogant faith in the idea that "I can't know if God exists." Faith in doubt. Then they stop looking for answers. They may continue to question, but their questions have no quest. They've decided to worship questions rather than use the tool for its intended purpose. Surely you've heard the expression "Thou shalt have no false gods." Doubt can become a false god. People have tremendous faith in this false god. They even worship it, have ceremonies about it. One could call it a religion of doubt.
Thomas: If there are ways to know if God exists, I'd like to explore them.
Monk: Good. I thought you would follow in the footsteps of the many great seekers who also bore the name Thomas.
Thomas: I'm in good company, am I?
Monk: If you only knew! Thomas Jefferson, the brilliant mind that authored the Declaration of Independence, pored over the words of Christ in the Gospels, on a quest to find the best way to live. Like

all of us, he also used the tool of questions to find what he wanted to find, not necessarily the whole truth.

Thomas: I didn't know that about Jefferson. What do you mean about not finding the whole truth?

Monk: The Gospels give us a glimpse of Christ's life but Jefferson made his own version. He carefully cut out sections with a scalpel. What sections? Sections that he didn't want to believe. Sections that made him uncomfortable! One historian joked that when Jefferson was done with Jesus, the Jesus that remained bore a striking resemblance to Thomas Jefferson!

Thomas: You have to be kidding me!

Monk: No. Look it up. Jefferson took what he liked and discarded what he didn't. It's a classic example of the choice we all have: either we are made in God's image or we make god – lower case "g" – in our image! Jefferson took that further than most, but, wouldn't you agree that we all do it in some area or another?

Thomas: I have to put some thought into that.

Monk: Back to your namesakes, there are a few additional Thomas's who might be very helpful to our quest.

Thomas: Can I stop you for a moment?

Monk: Certainly. What's on your mind?

Thomas: I'm surprised.

Monk: At what?

Thomas: More than surprised. But pleasantly. I can't believe I'm going to say this… I'm actually enjoying this conversation.

Monk: Well, that's just lovely to hear. [laughs a deep laugh]

Thomas: No, what I mean it this: I don't remember every really enjoying a conversation about religion anywhere near as much as I'm enjoying this back and forth.

Monk: That's great to hear, but unfortunate.

Thomas: Why?

Monk: It's unfortunate because conversations about important issues should happen much more often and should be enjoyable, at least to a degree.

Thomas: Only to a degree? Not too enjoyable?

Monk: Well, when you seek the truth, the journey is usually both comforting and discomforting. Comforting because you are looking for something so important and discomforting because it will demand something of you.

Thomas: In my experience, it's usually more uncomfortable. At least the conversations are.

Monk: I understand that. Perhaps we've forgotten the art behind good and meaningful conversation?

Thomas: Perhaps we don't even value good and meaningful conversation in today's culture!

Monk: There was another Thomas who did. He was once a topic of study in all the great centers of learning. Of course, that was a time when great ideas were measured by their merit, not their recency.

Thomas: Who is this Thomas?

Monk: Only one of the greatest minds in history, Thomas Aquinas.

Thomas: I've heard the name, but can't say that I know anything about him.

Monk: Aquinas was absolutely brilliant. He could write several books simultaneously. When he was a professor at the University of Paris, he held public discussions on some of humanity's most important questions. Today, you might call them town hall debates. Aquinas would take a question and mold it into its iron man form.

Thomas: Iron man?

Monk: The opposite of a "straw man." Rather than knocking down straw man arguments – the easiest version of the argument – he'd make challenges into their strongest form and build the debate, discussion and response around that.

Thomas: I like him so far.

Monk: In relation to our discussion, Aquinas debated some of the exact same things we're trying to figure out. He even said that the greatest charity we can do for others is to lead them to the truth. Notice that Aquinas didn't say smack them upside the head if they disagree with you. We can deeply enjoy a conversation if we are seeking what is. My job and yours, like Aquinas, is to be sheepdogs.

Thomas: Sheepdogs? Is that something Aquinas talked about?

Monk: No. That's from the monk. What does a sheepdog do?

Thomas: Got me! Bark, watch the sheep? Protect?

Monk: The sheepdog keeps the sheep following the shepherd. That's what Aquinas did. That's why he referred to Aristotle as the Holy Philosopher. Why? Aristotle sought to find, teach and live the truth. Where there is truth, it can only come from one place. Aristotle didn't know God as G-O-D, our God, but he was a sheepdog, trying to point others towards the truth. So many gurus today do the opposite. They get caught up in trying to be the shepherd. "Let me tell you my way" is their approach.

Thomas: What's wrong with that? Someone finds a way and shares it. That's a big deal for you?

Monk: No. The big deal is when they teach their way as the way, even when it is not.

Thomas: Hold on! Who's more guilty of that than you? [more than a slight agitation in his voice]

Monk: Whoa, cowboy, ayy? Are you a bit frustrated?

Thomas: More than a bit. All religious people like to say that their way is the only way.

Monk: All?

Thomas: Maybe not all, but your group is definitely guilty of this.

Monk: Thomas, remember the layers of stone in the Leaning Tower of Pisa?

Thomas: Sure.

Monk: Where would this question be on the tower?

Thomas: The one path to God question?

Monk: Yes.
Thomas: In the lower section. Maybe about 1/3 of the way up. I don't know.
Monk: Where would it fall in relation to the questions of "Does a creator exist?" and "What is the nature of that creator?"
Thomas: Those certainly come earlier. Does a creator exist comes before the nature of the creator, which comes before the "one path" question.
Monk: Agreed. With that being understood, should we try to handle our questions in the order of importance?
Thomas: Back to the "Prove to me that God exists!" then.
Monk: Sheepdog, Thomas, sheepdog. We're looking for the truth together. This discussion is not about one of us winning. We want the truth to win, at least that's been my assumption. Maybe that's why you say people don't talk about the important stuff anymore… it's become a "Prove it!" or "Convince me!" battle of ego.
Thomas: Sheepdog. Check. Searching for the shepherd of truth. Check. Carry on!
Monk: Aquinas outlined 5 proofs for the existence of God. His logic is profound yet, for the most part, simple. As another great thinker, Einstein, said… if you can't explain it to a 6-year-old, then you don't really understand it!
Thomas: Now you're comparing me to a 6-year-old?
Monk: Not at all. My apologies if it sounded that way. I'm simply saying that there's nothing wrong with simple explanations. Aquinas' first 3 proofs state that there must be an *unmoved mover*, an *uncaused cause*, and a *noncontingent being*. They go together. Do you remember Newton's laws from your schooling?
Thomas: An object at rest tends to stay at rest, an object in motion tends to stay in motion… that's one or Newton's laws, right?
Monk: Exactly! That's the unmoved mover. Imagine a group of children sitting in a big circle. They are instructed to tap the person to their right on the shoulder when – and only when – they are

tapped on the shoulder. Once one child is tapped, the tapping would theoretically go on forever. But the tapping would need to be started by an untapped tapper, an unmoved mover, a first motion. That is what we call God. The universe is in motion, therefore something untapped must have begun the motion. The uncaused cause is very similar. The cause that has always existed is what we call God. Third, everything we do and say is contingent upon something else. You live near the Hudson River. That mighty river is contingent upon streams feeding it, which are contingent upon precipitation falling, which is contingent upon evaporation, which is contingent upon sun and air, etc, etc. Can it go back forever? No. There had to be a first something that is not contingent upon anything. That is what we call God.

Thomas: The first 3 are very similar, and they make a lot of sense. Smart guy, this Aquinas! I'm surprised I've not heard these before.

Monk: Number 4… *Degrees of perfection*. If better exists, perfect must exist. Think of the most generous person you know. Is it possible to be more generous? Yes. How loving are you? Do you know people who are more loving that you? Degrees of perfection necessitate perfection. Perfect is what we call God. Number 5… *Design requires a designer*. Elon Musk's car is in orbit. Imagine an alien space craft visiting our solar system and finding that incredible piece of machinery in orbit. Would the aliens assume that it just "got there" or would they assume that it was designed by an intelligent designer? The more complex something is – here's degrees of perfection again – the more intelligence we can assume from the designer. The ultimate designer is what we call God.

Thomas: 5 proofs. Are there counter-arguments?

Monk: Certainly. There are counter arguments to every argument. However, I'd encourage you to listen very carefully when you hear a counter argument to these.

Thomas: Why?

Monk: Remember that questions are tools that can be used for many purposes. One of the most frequent uses of language is to justify what we've already decided to believe.

Thomas: Are there any more proofs?

Monk: Absolutely. There are dozens. Steve Jobs once invited the master cellist, Yo-Yo Ma, to perform for his birthday. Jobs described the music as the greatest argument he ever heard for the existence of God! Perfection. Beauty. Nature. Look at a leaf or a ladybug. Experience a sunset or full moon. Listen to bagpipes…

Thomas: Okay already! I get it. Lots of proofs. Do you have any favorites?

Monk: Presence.

Thomas: Presence?

Monk: Yes. Numina. The presence of a divine power.

Thomas: That's one of your favorite proofs for the existence of God? How so?

Monk: Let's try it this way. Have you ever had a feeling that something or someone was watching you? Or that you were not alone? Perhaps you were taking a walk in the woods or on a quiet road. Then you were overcome by a feeling that you were in the presence of someone else.

Thomas: Brother, are we getting into ghost stories now?

Monk: Funny, Thomas, but no. Very real. The essence of reality.

Thomas: I was kidding. Yes. Yes, I have felt that. I remember one occasion very clearly. I was staying at my parent's cabin in the Catskill Mountains of upstate New York. I was all alone in complete darkness. Heavy clouds blocked the moon and stars. There are no street lights on that country road. I stood at the top of the long winding driveway in silence when this eerie feeling came over me. I felt like something was out there. No, I *knew* something was out there. I turned on a flashlight and, sure enough, at the bottom of the driveway, across the small creek, I saw the reflection of two sets of eyes. Deer. Staring back at me. Something was there, alright.

Monk: That's presence. Something. Or someone.

Thomas: I don't see how that proves anything.

Monk: Throughout recorded history, people have known that there is something, really a someone, out there. They've tried to define that presence, that Numina. They've told stories about that Numina. They've created special days for that Numina.

Thomas: They just know?

Monk: They know. Something bigger, smarter, more capable, more perfect than them is out there.

Thomas: I see why you like this one.

Monk: G.K. Chesterton hinted at it when he mentioned the "Democracy of the Dead."

Thomas: The what?

Monk: Democracy of the Dead. Chesterton said we like to give everyone a vote except our parents. Those who came before us. When the democracy of the dead votes, we find that over 95% of all humanity has believed in some sort of Numina. Some presence that's bigger than we are. Something that we call God.

Thomas: But did generations past know as much as we do?

Monk: Know?

Thomas: You're talking about people who didn't have a clue about all the science and technology we have today.

Monk: What difference does that make?

Thomas: They just didn't know what we know.

Monk: Thomas, what's the difference between knowledge and wisdom?

Thomas: Knowledge is having information. Wisdom is knowing what to do with that information.

Monk: Good. Nuclear capability gives us a great example of the difference. Knowledge allows us to split the atom. Wisdom helps guide us with what should be done with that knowledge. Again, a tool. We can do great good or great evil with that tool, with all the tools this knowledge facilitates. Einstein put it this way: "I know not with what weapons World War III will be fought, but World War IV will be fought with sticks and stones." We have the knowledge to end civilization as we know it. But will we exercise the wisdom not to?

Thomas: That's a powerful distinction. It reminds me of Pandora's Box. Knowledge of what's inside or how to open it is not the same as the wisdom to discern whether or not to open it and what to do with the contents if we do choose to open it.

Monk: There you have it.

Thomas: You were saying that throughout history, humanity has just known that there was something, or someone, out there?

Monk: It's one of the reasons we are deathly afraid of silence.

Thomas: Why do you say that?

Monk: We know that in the silence we may encounter that something or someone, that Numina. And, more than that, we have a feeling that it will demand something of us. That it will change us.

Thomas: Change us? Demand something?

Monk: Sure. We fear that the Numina will give us a glimpse of who we are capable of becoming. It's why, throughout history, only the most courageous are willing to spend considerable time in silence, in prayer, in meditation, in contemplation with the Presence, with the Numina, with God. We fear that His presence will change us, call us to confront the false self. Shows us a glimpse of our true self. That scares us to death.

Thomas: We know there's something out there. We know it's bigger than us. And we're afraid?

Monk: Deathly afraid.

Thomas: I can buy that. So God's a God of fear?

Monk: No. We are creatures who choose to respond with fear.

Thomas: But God made us that way.

Monk: No. He made us in His image.

Thomas: And we have fear? So He…

Monk: No. He wants us to step into His presence and he whispers these words to us over and over: "Let me love you. Let me love you. Let me love you."

Thomas: That's different from "Let me change you."

Monk: Very good observation, Thomas.

Thomas: We fear the quiet, the solitude, the… what did you call it?

Monk: Contemplation.

Thomas: … and this Numina simply asks that we let Him love us?

Monk: He whispers these words because we are not convinced that we are worthy of His love. It's a love we can't describe. Sure, the greatest poets and psalmists have tried throughout the centuries, but this… this is a love so deep, so complete… How can I… deserve… this?

Thomas: Can we?

Monk: No. That's why He whispers it and we so frequently run away. We hide. We refuse to believe that we, little old monk… or little old Thomas, can be worthy of that depth, that unconditional love.

Thomas: But does the other stuff happen to?

Monk: What other stuff?

Thomas: The demands. The expectation of change?

Monk: Oh yeah.

Thomas: Are we right to be afraid then?

Monk: Yes. And no.

Thomas: Oh, come on!

Monk: Well, the answer depends on who we believe.

Thomas: Who we believe?

Monk: Certainly. The world gives us one answer. God gives us the opposite answer.

Thomas: Which is?

Monk: Fear not. Be not afraid.

Thomas: Really? Why would God tell us this?

Monk: Because He knows that we are.

5. Only One Path to God? Really? *Seems Arrogant!*

Thomas: You've found the way to God! Isn't it beyond arrogant to make that kind of a claim?

Monk: Humble, not arrogant. They're opposites.

Thomas: People who say "Your way is wrong. My way is the only way" are *humble*? I can't wait to hear this explanation.

Monk: We have essentially two options here. Either the path to God is manmade or God-made. If it's God-made, then it's humble to follow it. If manmade, then it could very well be arrogant for one man to claim that his way was better than another.

Thomas: Let's explore your truth, then.

Monk: No.

Thomas: No?

Monk: No. *Your* truth? This does not exist. Thomas, do words matter?

Thomas: Naturally.

Monk: Naturally. Good. What does the word "truth" mean?

Thomas: What we believe to be true or correct.

Monk: It does?

Thomas: Yes.

Monk: No.

Thomas: No?

Monk: Your definition of truth is not true.

Thomas: Clever. Meaning what?

Monk: Meaning the word *truth* does not mean what *we believe*! Do you care to try again?

Thomas: I think I'll go with what you said earlier. What is. Truth is what is.

Monk: And you're sure about this?

Thomas: I am.

Monk: Then you see why these expressions "your truth" and "my truth" are nonsensical?
Thomas: Not entirely.
Monk: Can you give me an example of one of these "your truths."
Thomas: Speak your truth! Share your truth. Have the courage to go public with your truth. These are all common expressions.
Monk: I've heard them, but can you give me some context?
Thomas: You bet! A celebrity recently, I think it was at some awards banquet, said, "Speaking your truth is the most powerful tool we have."
Monk: Hold on! You're giving me a quote from a celebrity at an awards banquet? This is the example you chose in a conversation about the meaning of truth?
Thomas: Hear me out, please, Brother!
Monk: I'll try. It may be very difficult, but I'll try.
Thomas: Why difficult?
Monk: Popularity and truth are rarely aligned. It's one of the devil's oldest tricks, whispering into our ears about the popular thing to do or say… If popular people use an expression like "your truth" often enough, are we wise to assume that this nonsensical phrase has some meaning? Or are we fools? Should we base what we believe on a popularity contest? You're familiar with the expression, "A thousand lemmings can't be wrong"?
Thomas: You're a little excited about this. It's just a phrase.
Monk: Just a phrase? Just… a… Phrase? Thomas, a phrase that misleads millions of people is "just a phrase!" Pontius Pilate and the Romans misled with a phrase. At His trial, Christ tells the Roman ruler, Pontius Pilate, "For this I was born and for this I came into the world, to testify to the truth. Everyone who belongs to the truth listens to my voice." The Truth, Thomas, not his truth, not your truth. THE Truth. To which this celebrity… I mean Pilate… responded – and we can safely assume quite sarcastically, "What is truth?" In other words, we can have all different truths. When

people with power (like Pilate) or popularity (like this celebrity you referenced) teach something so incorrect, they have the potential to mislead the hearts and souls of generations. You do see why this is not "just a phrase?"

Thomas: Fair enough. But who are you to say that they are misleading hearts and souls?

Monk: The words, my dear Thomas. We've defined truth as what is. I have a Godson who is 8-years-old. That is what is. The truth. He might feel like he's old enough to drive the car and a baby-sitter might say he's behaving like a two-year-old when he doesn't get his way. But those are opinions about what is. Your opinion and my opinion. Your experience and my experience. Not your truth or my truth.

Thomas: What should this celebrity have said instead, assuming she were stuck in a cabin in a snowstorm with a monk for a long time before that speech?

Monk: Your celebrity could use a slightly modified statement: Speaking the truth is one of the most powerful tools we have. How's that?

Thomas: Fine. Can we get back to the question now?

Monk: The question. I like the way you phrased that. It is the question, or at least one of THE questions. Saint Benedict says, "He should only be admitted to the monastery who truly seeks God." The only criteria. Doesn't have to have a resume, doesn't have to have a letter of recommendation. Does he truly seek God? Because then we can do that together and do something beautiful for God, as Mother Teresa so often said. Make something wonderous happen. What are you seeking? What are you looking for? And that's a question we can honestly ask throughout our lives. The reason you are asking the question, Thomas, is that you're just not satisfied with where you are with God. And you can't be. There is no…

Thomas: How do you know I'm not satisfied with… how'd you put it?

Monk: …satisfied with your relationship with your God.

Thomas: How could you know that?

Monk: None of us are. How could we be?

Thomas: I am.

Monk: You are?

Thomas: Yes.

Monk: Are you the same Thomas who, just a few minutes ago wasn't even sure if God exists?

Thomas: That's me.

Monk: And now you're satisfied with your relationship with your God? Could you tell me a little about that relationship, perhaps describe that relationship?

Thomas: I wouldn't use your word, relationship.

Monk: Why not?

Thomas: It's nonexistent. There is no relationship. But I'm satisfied.

Monk: Then we're all set here.

Thomas: You're good with that?

Monk: As I mentioned, Saint Benedict was always asking, "Do you seek God?" If the answer is no, then we are okay.

Thomas: You're okay with my answer?

Monk: The Living God, the God who knows more about you than you know about you, the God whose love you've only sampled in the briefest of moments in your life, the God who spun the universe off of His fingertips, the God who created not just life, but the possibility of life, not just humanity but the unique human being that is you. The God who exists outside of space and time, the God who desires, above all else, to have a personal relationship with you! The God who loves you enough to give you the freedom to decide whether or not you'll enter into that relationship. This God…

Thomas: This God sounds too good to be true.

Monk: It's too good to be made up!

Thomas: You said that before.

Monk: And I'll probably say it again. What if this God is true? Would your answer still hold that you're content to not have a relationship with this God? Would you still answer that you don't seek this God?

Thomas: I can't believe I'm saying this, but I believe you'd have to be a fool not to seek a God like the one you've described… how could I be content not to have a relationship with such a God, if a relationship were possible?

Monk: Should we go back to the question, then?

Thomas: Let's do that.

Monk: Did you know, Thomas, that the early Christians, the early followers of Christ, were known as "Followers of the Way."

Thomas: The way?

Monk: Christ himself said it, "I am the way, the truth, and the life."

Thomas: One way. As in the only way? Or one of several ways? A way?

Monk: God's ways and man's ways are not the same.

Thomas: I think I'll have to agree with you there. That might actually be the only thing we can be absolutely certain of in this entire conversation!

Monk: Once again you're in good company.

Thomas: How so?

Monk: We do not see things the same way God does. The wisest among us have said this since the beginning of time. The prophet, Isaiah, put it this way: "For my thoughts are not your thoughts, nor are your ways my ways, says the LORD. For as the heavens are higher than the earth, so are my ways higher than your ways, my thoughts higher than your thoughts."

Thomas: That's a good way to put it, but… doesn't that support my point? If we can't really know God's ways, how can we know the one way – if there is just one as you claim – to God?

Monk: We're getting there. Think back to our discussion about travelling to Rome.

Thomas: Are we going there again?

Monk: I'd love to! The great churches in Rome – throughout Italy for that matter – are full of clues about the path to and the nature of God. But Rome, ah, Rome! What's that expression? About the roads?

Thomas: ...they lead to Rome! All roads lead to Rome! Yes, of course they do. The Romans conquered every neighbor that they could and built roads leading to Rome.

Monk: But all roads surely do NOT lead to Rome!

Thomas: Another expression. You get hung up on a lot of those, don't you?

Monk: When the expression misleads hearts, minds, and souls, yes! In particular, souls. If an expression leads just a single soul down the wrong path, the impact of the faulty expression is infinite.

Thomas: Infinite? Come on, now.

Monk: Infinite. Because your soul, Thomas, is infinite.

Thomas: Fine. The words are a big deal because of their impact. The expression's wrong.

Monk: Some roads do lead to Rome. Many do. Many do not. Some that do lead to Rome are dangerous, crowded, slow, filled with traffic or potholes or distractions. Or all of the above. Some highways lead directly to Rome, but... And this is a big but... Could a car be driving 80 mph on a highway but be headed in the exact opposite direction, away from Rome? Each minute has that driver further from Rome, not closer.

Thomas: That's great. But your analogy works the other way around, too. Thousands – no, hundreds of thousands – of roads will get you to Rome. You have to start where you are, on the road you're on. What say ye to that, monk?

Monk: Very good. I agree.

Thomas: What? You do? I thought...

Monk: You thought that I would say only one road works?

Thomas: Uh, yeah! Isn't that what you say?

Monk: No.
Thomas: So we agree here? Not all roads, but many roads lead to Rome? Like ancient Rome, there is not just one road, or path, or way to God! Amen, Brother!
Monk: Do we agree? I think there are several conclusions we can make from this analogy.
Thomas: Yes?
Monk: First: That not all roads, paths, or ways, lead to God. Just as some roads lead us away from Rome, some paths lead us away from God. Second: Some roads are better than others. Third: Some roads do lead to God.
Thomas: Let me see if I buy that. Some roads do lead to God, some don't, and some are better than others. Did I capture it?
Monk: You did.
Thomas: Well then, help me understand your one way idea.
Monk: It's not my idea. It's His.
Thomas: I see. But his ways are not the same as your ways.
Monk: Correct. You're good. As high as the heavens are above the earth, so high are His ways above my ways. But that doesn't change what the Christ told us.
Thomas: That he's the way?
Monk: That He, The Christ, is THE way! And that no one comes to the Father except through Christ. It's a "this road works. No other road works" proposition.
Thomas: Exclusive. That's what I can't believe.
Monk: Can't believe or don't want to believe?
Thomas: Both. It's either Jesus or nothing. I don't like your options.
Monk: They're not my options. They're His.
Thomas: Don't like them.
Monk: Talk to Him about that.
Thomas: Maybe I will.
Monk: Good. I highly recommend it. Wrestle with your God.

Thomas: Wrestle?

Monk: Israel. The word means "one who wrestles with God." Wrestle with God about your disagreement. Only do me one favor.

Thomas: What favor?

Monk: Invite God to the wrestling match. The Bible is full of stories about people who wrestle with God. Abraham argues with God about how many good people have to live in a town for the town to be worth saving. Job wrestles with God about the existence of pain and suffering in the world, more specifically in his own life. Jonah wrestles with God and runs in the exact opposite direction of God. Then he wants God to punish the people who repent. Wrestle with God! You're in great company. Go ahead and wrestle. Ask your God about this one way. Seek an answer.

Thomas: I might take you up on that.

Monk: You might? Okay. I'll accept that promise.

Thomas: For now, can we stop for a taste of that soup you have cooking on the stove?

Monk: Do you hunger?

6. Is Socrates in Heaven?

Thomas: Delicious! Truly delicious.

Monk: Hmmm. [nods his head] Truly.

Thomas: I was thinking while we devoured your soup.

Monk: Good thoughts?

Thomas: Very good. To go with the very good soup!

Monk: Good? What is good?

Thomas: What do you mean?

Monk: Never mind. I was just thinking about another conversation.

Thomas: Is Socrates in Heaven? Does Socrates find God?

Monk: Whoa! Did I just get a serious promotion? I decide who's to enter Heaven now? Have I been handed the keys to eternal life?

Thomas: You know what I mean.

Monk: Do I? Then maybe.

Thomas: Maybe what?

Monk: Maybe Socrates is in Heaven.

Thomas: You're not sure? If there's only one way, if one road leads to God and no other road leads to God, shouldn't you be able to answer the question with a yes or no?

Monk: Yes. And no.

Thomas: Why do I engage with you?

Monk: How long must you put up with me! We're stuck here, remember? You have no choice! Consider it a gift from God.

Thomas: A gift, why?

Monk: You have questions that deserve answers. God gives each of us the chance to seek and find answers to the most important questions. Our time together may just help each of us get closer to God. If that's not a gift, I don't know what is.

Thomas: We answer one question and find that two or three more have popped up.

Monk: Socrates had similar experiences in his quest for truth.

Thomas: Did he find it? Did Socrates get in to Heaven?

Monk: That answer, that decision, is above my pay grade.
Thomas: But you must have an opinion on the matter?
Monk: Opinion? From what I know of Socrates, I would most certainly expect to meet him in Heaven. But I have no way of knowing his heart, his true motives. Only God knows that. And He has the final say. If Socrates truly sought to find and live truth… From Plato's writings about Socrates, he appears to have pure motives. But you and I know that we can fool some people sometimes…
Thomas: …but you can't fool all the people all the time! Sing it, Monk!
Monk: Ha! Have you ever experienced what appeared to be a pure motive, only to later find that you'd been tricked?
Thomas: Certainly! Now Socrates was put on trial, if I recall, for corrupting the youth of Athens and for being an atheist.
Monk: Correct. He didn't believe in or follow the gods of the state.
Thomas: It wasn't that he didn't believe in a higher power, it was…
Monk: He spoke about the "Unknown God" is how Socrates put it.
Thomas: Unknown God?
Monk: Yes. Did your philosophy professor forgot to mention this?
Thomas: I certainly don't remember covering it.
Monk: Much like Thomas Jefferson cutting out segments of the Gospels, we are all tempted to skip over or cut out things that we find uncomfortable.
Thomas: Tell me more about this Unknown God.
Monk: Socrates' Unknown God may not be referring to another god… Don't forget that Socrates never uses the plural.
Thomas: Go on.
Monk: For him, there is one God. He's not saying, like the Apostle Paul did, that there's an unknown god among your pantheon that you're not serving. What he's saying is that you don't know the real one. The unknown god is the only God. At least that's the interpretation Christianity placed on it later on.

Thomas: Makes sense. So Socrates could've been killed partly because he believed in God? They said he was an atheist because he didn't believe in their gods. He could've been killed, really, because he was convinced that their gods were not real.
Monk: Which is the same thing.
Thomas: … and that there was a real God.
Monk: Right. A God that's bigger, a God who created everything.
Thomas: So does he get to Heaven, then? Socrates?
Monk: Um. On the principle of conscience?
Thomas: Yeah.
Monk: Yes. If he had known Jesus Christ, had the opportunity to believe in Jesus Christ, would he have believed in Jesus Christ? Yes.
Thomas: Okay. Got it.
Monk: That's the whole principle.
Thomas: If he had the opportunity to believe in Jesus, would he?
Monk: Yes.
Thomas: I put it this way, and maybe this is completely off. If you seek truth – try to find it and then try to live it, is that a good way to put it?
Monk: That is the definition of conscience.
Thomas: Seek and you'll find.
Monk: Here's the classic example. There's a guy in India. He believes in gods with 12 arms and all kinds of stuff. He is faithful to his wife, an excellent father, he follows the truth – as he *understands* the truth. He, for any one of a number of reasons, does not know Jesus Christ. Given the poor example of the way Christians have treated one another and treated the rest of the world, he has no incentive by looking at Christians to believe in Jesus Christ.
Thomas: That makes sense. And?
Monk: He is living the truth. Then how is it, if we have to be saved through Jesus Christ, how is it that he can be saved in Catholic doctrine? Very simple. Jesus says, "I am the way, the truth, and the

life." He doesn't say you've got to spell truth J-E-S-U-S C-H-R-I-S-T. Since Jesus redeemed the *whole* world. He didn't save the whole world. He redeemed the whole world. Meaning He bought them back. So their goodness, their acceptance…

Thomas: They're justified…

Monk: No. No, no, no, no! You anticipate the answer! It means that…

Thomas: … they're paid for. They're redeemed.

Monk: NO! It means that because of the blood of Christ, any good act, any truth, is acceptable to God the Father because that person is made by God the Father. The person is redeemed by Jesus Christ. Their actions, their goodness, is acceptable to God the Father only through Jesus Christ. They're following the truth, then they can't be other than Jesus Christ. Does this man sin? I'm sure he does. That's not the point. The point is his fundamental option is to live the truth in integrity. And that can only come from the Holy Spirit.

Thomas: This man… he'll never make confession. He may never even say the word "Jesus" or even hear of Jesus.

Monk: But he's saved by Jesus, none the less.

Thomas: He'll never participate in a Sacrament, which is…

Monk: Which is the ultimate for a Christian.

Thomas: The more you know of the truth, the more responsible you are?

Monk: Right. The way one of the famous monks puts it is, "We participate in the banquet of the Lord's wedding feast. Here. On earth. In the Eucharist. They have to wait until they get to heaven for the banquet. But they will be welcome there."

Thomas: The devil's advocate question seems to be this: the easier way is to grow up somewhere else.

Monk: No. Because that's not invincible ignorance. That's deliberate. And that sends you to Hell.

Thomas: Oh wow.

Monk: Faith is necessary to be saved. God wants everyone to be saved, so God gives everyone the same amount of faith. Francis of Assisi doesn't have any more faith than you or I do. So if you refuse to believe, it's your choice.
Thomas: It's not God's fault?
Monk: Right. You've been given the same opportunity to believe…
Thomas: Which means no matter what life you live, you're exposed to enough of the truth to respond to it?
Monk: No matter what life you live, the image of God dwells in you, no matter what your external circumstances are.
Thomas: So, is this truth, this image of God, written in our consciences? To know what's right and wrong?
Monk: God says, "I will write it in their hearts, if they trust me. They will not need a teacher because I will be their teacher." Given, of course, if they choose to believe in Him. Otherwise, why would they want Him to teach them?
Thomas: Hmmm.
Monk: There are those people who run around trying to find as many people as agree with them on an individual issue. They collectively call something the truth because they've all decided it was true, without reference to anything objective.
Thomas: If I can get a few people to agree with me, then we can create the truth? Is that the approach?
Monk: That's where movements and ideologies are born. You've got to misunderstand this the same way I do, or else you're not allowed to believe in anything.
Thomas: It's people looking for an answer that's not the one they've been given?
Monk: They might be looking for an answer that aligns with what they've already decided they're going to do. An easier answer. An answer that doesn't demand anything, that doesn't require anything. No matter how crazy.

7. What's up with all the Rules?

Jesus said unto him, "Thou shalt love the Lord thy God with all thy heart, and with all thy soul, and with all thy mind. This is the first and great commandment. And the second is like unto it, Thou shalt love thy neighbor as thyself. On these two commandments hang all the law and the prophets."

Thomas: What's up with all the rules?
Monk: What rules?
Thomas: Oh come on! Everywhere you turn, there's another rule.
Monk: Really? Please do explain.
Thomas: Well, all the regular rules… "Don't kill", "Don't steal." But then there's all the extra stuff piled on. "Go to church on Sundays", "Don't eat certain foods", "Rest on Sundays", and a lot of rules about sex, yes?
Monk: Ah, those rules! What about them?
Thomas: Too many, for starters. And too much control.
Monk: How many is too many?
Thomas: Oh I don't know. Maybe ten or twenty would be enough. Any more than that would be too many.
Monk: And you're saying that the church has more than that?
Thomas: Are you kidding me? Way more than 20. I bet it's more than 200.
Monk: Ten or twenty would be ideal?
Thomas: I don't have an exact number, but you understand what I'm saying.
Monk: I do. Remember the story of Adam and Eve?
Thomas: With the apple in the garden? Sure. What about it?
Monk: How many rules did God give them?
Thomas: Well they… don't eat the apple. Was it only that one rule?
Monk: One rule.
Thomas: And?

Monk: How'd they do with that one rule?

Thomas: Terrible.

Monk: Right.

Thomas: Are you suggesting that more rules is better? That we are more likely to follow more rules than less?

Monk: Not at all. What was the purpose of that one rule?

Thomas: The purpose? God's in charge. Do as he says. Don't eat the apple because you'll be powerful like God. You'll know good and evil.

Monk: No. That's not what God says.

Thomas: Then where did I get that?

Monk: The serpent said that. The father of lies said that.

Thomas: What does God say?

Monk: God says that you'll die.

Thomas: There you go. Unrealistic. Unfair. Why should they die just for eating a delicious piece of fruit?

Monk: There you go, quoting the serpent again. God's unfair, unrealistic, the apple's good for you. Look at it! Don't you want to take a bite?

Thomas: This is so wrong?

Monk: One rule. Anything else in the garden they could eat. Not the fruit of that one tree. Listen to me, Thomas! Whatever that one rule was, the serpent's strategy would have been similar. God is unrealistic. God is unfair. Demanding. Disobey God. You'll like it. You'll enjoy it. You'll be like God if you do. Who is God to try to run your life? The serpent was whispering, even back then, "What's up with all the rules?"

Thomas: But there was only one rule.

Monk: We've been through that part already, but how did they do with that one rule?

Thomas: Horribly.

Monk: Right. Let's see if we can figure out the purpose of that rule, shall we?

Thomas: I'll bite that apple!

Monk: Clever. Christ was once asked which rule was the most important. By that time, the Jewish people had 613 rules.

Thomas: 613! Even more than 10 0r 20 – or even 200. Too many!

Monk: Jesus' answer suggests that He would be on your side in this.

Thomas: He would? So I'm right then, your church has too many rules!

Monk: The apple, Thomas, the apple! Look away from the apple!

Thomas: What?

Monk: God, in the garden, gave one rule. But you and I, we stare at that one thing we're not allowed to do until we're obsessed with doing it. One rule, Thomas!

Thomas: You said Jesus would be on my side in this? It sounds like you are, too.

Monk: Jesus was asked, what's the most important rule. He answered with one rule. Love God above all, with your whole heart, mind, soul. In other words, with everything you've got. If you give everything, what do you have left?

Thomas: Nothing.

Monk: Right. So we have one rule. But then Christ follows up with a second rule. Love your neighbor as yourself. That's it.

Thomas: That's it? Two rules then?

Monk: Really just one. Love God with everything you've got. By default then, you would love His creation.

Thomas: So 1 rule, not 10 - or 20 - or 200.

Monk: Or 613!

Thomas: Simple. Then where do all the rules come from?

Monk: All the rules exist to protect the ultimate relationship, the relationship we have with God and His creation. That's the prime directive. Love of God, Love of neighbor. From there, every other regulation flows. Throw it up against that. Does it serve the prime directive – I sound like Captain Kirk over here – but does it serve the prime directive? Or doesn't it?

Thomas: A monk quoting Star Trek. Did I really just hear that?

Monk: Yeah, you did. Prime Directive is a helpful way to look at it. The law of Moses is every one of the commandments followed by "Why shouldn't I kill?" Because love doesn't kill. Why shouldn't I lie? Because love doesn't lie. Killing God's creation certainly damages the relationship we have with our Creator. Lying damages that relationship. Love makes time to nurture relationship, therefore honor the Sabbath. Take time out to be with your God, your family, and your neighbors. Every rule has clear application to the relationship we have with our Creator and His creation.

Thomas: All of them – all of the rules – protect a relationship?

Monk: Yeah.

Thomas: That's the Ten Commandments. What about other rules?

Monk: Those are just elaborations on the original 10.

Thomas: Fasting? How's that an elaboration of the original 10?

Monk: Forget the 10, let's just stick with Christ's shortened version. Love God. Love neighbor. Giving anything requires that you have it to give. *Nemo dat quod non habet!* You can't give what you don't have.

Thomas: So when I fast I'll have more food to share with my neighbor?

Monk: No! It's not about the food. It's about something bigger than that. Self-control. You can't give of yourself if you don't possess yourself. You need the ability to control yourself in order to choose to give of yourself. Love is a verb. It's an active choice. Love chooses to share, chooses to forgive, chooses to want what's best for the other. In a culture dominated by "what's in it for me?" how can we preserve the right relationship between ourselves and food? Fast. The practice of fasting strengthens the muscle of self-control.

Thomas: Fasting leads to more self-control. That simple. I've never looked at it from that angle.

Monk: It's similar to biting your tongue. Surely you remember the little rabbit in Bambi? If you can't say somethin' nice…

Thomas: …don't say nuthin' at all!

Monk: Self-control allows the possibility of self-less love. If fasting, refraining from eating, is a challenge, try refraining from complaining or criticizing or lusting!

Thomas: Is every single rule designed to protect relationships? Relationship with God, with others, with life?

Monk: The right relationship, yes. If you're talking about family, you got a 4th Commandment… "Honor your mother and father." The Church asks, what is meant by the 4th Commandment? Obey all lawful authority that is not evil, that is not asking something that is against the other 9 Commandments.

Thomas: Hmmm.

Monk: Relationships are intertwined. Like Saint Francis said, "He who offends against one virtue offends against all."

Thomas: Thou shalt not covet. I never liked that one.

Monk: I suspect not. Maybe that's why it's spelled out. We like to covet.

Thomas: I suppose it makes sense in your context.

Monk: It's not my context, Thomas. It's God's.

Thomas: Well, the rules make sense when they exist for one purpose: to protect relationship. But aren't there still times when we don't know the right thing? What then?

Monk: God's given you the most wonderful gifts to deal with this.

Thomas: Conscience? So let your conscience be your guide?

Monk: His Word, His Son, His Church. His prophets. His saints. Add reason and yes, add conscience to that. But "Let your conscience be your guide?" No! Let your *formed conscience* be your guide.

Thomas: Formed conscience? I'm not okay with just my plain old conscience?

Monk: How often do you listen to that *plain old conscience* of yours? Is it exercised regularly? Or have you become adept at ignoring it? Think of a runner who never times a race or an athlete who never competes against live opponents. We need to train against the truth.

Thomas: So formed is another way of saying trained, in good shape?

Monk: Consistent. Measured against something absolute. This might be another conversation for another time. Let's get back to the Prime Directive. That's absolute. Love the Creator. Love His creation, which includes your neighbor. Chesterton said that we are to love our neighbors, and love our enemies; probably because generally they are the same people. You've got to read some Chesterton. You'd love his wisdom and humor. Will you?

Thomas: I think I will.

Monk: Good. You won't be disappointed. Iron sharpens iron.

Thomas: Can't argue there! I enjoy reading authors who have thought long and hard about important questions.

Monk: That's part of what I meant by a formed conscience. Testing your will against truth. But beware. If Christ hasn't made you uncomfortable recently, be careful! It may not be Christ's voice you're listening to. It's like exercising with some resistance. Or competing against the best. It strengthens us, molds us, but we don't always feel good in the process!

Thomas: So two truths. Two rules. Love God. Love neighbor.

Monk: If it doesn't serve the prime directive, why doesn't it? Because it doesn't apply to you? Because a circumstance is different? You can't just throw the rule away or you're risking the relationship that it's there to protect. Thou shalt not kill. Saint Augustine put it so simply: "Love God and do what you will!"

Thomas: I like that. Pretty simple. Love God and do whatever you want.

Monk: No, Thomas! Not whatever you want. What you will – as in what you choose. Will as in will power. As in choosing even when it's not what you *want* to choose, not what you may feel like in the moment!

Thomas: So Augustine was saying to love God and then choose to do what someone who loves God would choose to do.

Monk: There you go. Choose. Choosing to love God leads to choosing to love his creation which leads to…

Thomas: …the Golden Rule! Treating others the way you want to be treated. So choosing to love means never choosing to kill, lie, steal – all that. But never?

Monk: Well, if some guy wants to kill my family. We're not talking about a rule here, we're talking about a relationship… which defines the rule, defines the circumstances of the rule.

Thomas: Uh huh.

Monk: It's not situational ethics. Because there are principles that guide it, not just the situation or how you're feeling in that moment. Like Sergeant Giraci used to say: "Never aim a gun at a constipated police officer."

Thomas: Who? What? What does that mean? [Laughter] Moving right along then… Is the Bible consistent on this? Did the Old Testament capture the "Love your neighbor" the way you're describing it?

Monk: Oh yeah. Jesus was quoting Moses.

Thomas: He was?

Monk: The Book of Deuteronomy: "Hear O Israel, the Lord your God is One. The Lord alone. You must love the Lord your God with your whole mind, your heart, and your soul. And you must love your neighbor as yourself."

Thomas: So it's not a new thing that Jesus teaches?

Monk: Not at all. Just providing clarity and a reminder.

Thomas: All the other rules come from this, as you call it, the prime directive?

Monk: Yes. Except the rules we make up.

Thomas: That's it! That's what I'm getting at. All the rules that we make up. For example, I've met a lot of people in charge of religious education programs who are very big on their rules. If you don't sign up on time, or if you miss a class, if you haven't...

Monk: Hold on! I make a distinction between rules and paperwork.

Thomas: Okay. That doesn't even fit under rules, it's just paperwork?

Monk: Just paperwork.

Thomas: Just garbage, extra junk?

Monk: Yes. To keep somebody happy! Maybe herself, maybe her boss.

Thomas: So the rules there would be "What matters? What really matters? What are we learning?" That's where a real rule should fit. But relationship is still the basis for those rules... Brother, I'm not sold on this idea just yet. I don't see a hole in what you're saying, but there must be one.

Monk: I see. You're looking for holes. Thomas, ask yourself, "Why am I looking for holes?"

Thomas: I shouldn't look for holes? Blind faith in an idea?

Monk: Is that what I said?

Thomas: Pretty much.

Monk: Not pretty much. Did you hear my question?

Thomas: Which one? Why am I looking for holes?

Monk: That's the one!

Thomas: Shouldn't I look for holes?

Monk: Should you?

Thomas: Yes.

Monk: Why?

Thomas: To see... Oh! I get it. You keep going back to *Why?* You're asking about my motivation. *Why* am I looking for holes?

Monk: Hmmmm! That was the question.

Thomas: I'm looking because I'm not convinced. I want to test your theory about rules protecting relationship.

Monk: And you want to be convinced? Once again, you can question because you want to find truth and follow it. Or… you can question as a distraction, you can question with no intention of finding or following. You can make your questions your excuse for not following things you already know to be true. Questions are a tool. We can use them to seek answers or arguments – reasons or excuses! Why are you looking for holes, Thomas?

Thomas: Oh. I suppose, if I'm honest, I have to admit that I don't really want to be convinced. I'd like some of the rules to just be arbitrary.

Monk: If you're honest, indeed! Why would you chose to not be honest with yourself? Forget that question. What's the advantage of arbitrary rules?

Thomas: Let's keep this honesty thing going, shall we? Why would anyone prefer arbitrary rules? If the rules are arbitrary, we don't have to follow them.

Monk: Ah… we're getting somewhere. What happens to a baseball game if a player, or an entire team, decide not to follow some of the rules?

Thomas: The game wouldn't work. To use your concept of protecting relationship, the relationship between the teams – and even between the fans and the game itself – would break down.

Monk: Not my concept, Thomas. God's! Or in this example, your baseball gods! So the rules of baseball help to protect relationship?

Thomas: I suppose.

Monk: And if a rule were changed in the middle of a game?

Thomas: The game would suffer. All the relationships between fans, players, and teams would suffer.

Monk: So clear rules serve the prime directive, the ultimate purpose?

Thomas: I suppose so. Relationships don't seem to be as important in the current culture. People's lives are full of anxiety, depression, lack of a sense of purpose. I read a study about the low Emotional Intelligence in the modern world. Two of the biggest driving factors: we've gotten rid of spirituality and we've gotten rid of the family unit. Two things bigger than the individual that we could count on.

Monk: And that was the plan of the Devil from the beginning. Don't forget, the first thing that Satan did is interrupt the relationship between God and man. Then, relationship between Eve and Adam. Thomas, are you willing to take a hard look at which rules you don't want to follow? And the relationships meant to be protected by those rules?

Thomas: Are you assuming that I ignore what I know to be right in some area of my life?

Monk: Not at all. My apologies. It's no assumption and I didn't even mean to direct it at you. Allow me to rephrase. Am *I* willing to take a hard look at the rules I don't want to follow? And the ramification on my relationships with God and His creation? I say it's no assumption because it's an obvious truth about our human nature: we have a tendency to hide from that which might be uncomfortable.

Thomas: Can you give me an example?

Monk: I'd rather not!

Thomas: Ha! Now you're hiding from… how'd you put it: that which might be uncomfortable!

Monk: It is funny, but at the same time very serious. Confession is probably the easiest example I can give you. Who among us likes to confess his sins? To make an accounting of my poor choices – in my thoughts and in my words… in what I have done and in what I have failed to do, to own up to being responsible for making those choices – usually repeatedly? To own it. To say aloud, it was my own fault. To say "I messed up." To seek forgiveness?

Thomas: I wondered how long it would be before you brought that up!
Monk: You and me, both!
Thomas: So that's a challenge, even for the monk?
Monk: Naturally. But look at the rule in relation to the prime directive.
Thomas: It makes sense on an entirely different level. My relationship with my God is not as good as it could be. I accept responsibility for my short-comings and ask for forgiveness.
Monk: Yes.
Thomas: But why go to a priest?
Monk: Why, indeed?
Thomas: I guess we can look to your… I mean God's prime directive! Love of God, love of His creation. Relationship with God, relationship with His creation. Would this "go to confession" rule help protect those?
Monk: Would it?
Thomas: [Silence, looks down.]
Monk: What's on your mind?
Thomas: I don't like the answer. It's clear, but I don't want to talk about it.
Monk: I see.
Thomas: Good for you. I don't want to see!
Monk: Let Him love you.
Thomas: What?
Monk: Let Him love you!
Thomas: Meaning?
Monk: Let the God of the universe, the God who had you in mind when He created you, the God who knows you better than you can ever know yourself… let Him love you! Right where you are and as you are. In your thoughts and words. In what you've done and failed to do. In your best and worst decisions. Just let Him love you.

Thomas: I… like that. It makes sense. But I don't know how loveable I am.
Monk: Infinitely. To an infinite God, who is the essence of love. Yes, Thomas! Just let Him love you. Stop with your reasons that He can't or won't.
Thomas: But I…
Monk: But nothing! There is nothing you can do to stop that love.
Thomas: I have so many reasons for not doing what I know I should.
Monk: Of course you do. So do I. You're unique, but not in that!
Thomas: Thanks, I think.
Monk: Does it – confession – help protect one of those prime directive relationships?
Thomas: Of course it does. Apologizing, accepting responsibility, telling another person, telling God. It just doesn't feel good.
Monk: Feeling good and doing good are not the same.
Thomas: You can say that again.
Monk: Feeling good and doing good…
Thomas: I got it, Brother.
Monk: Yeah, you got it alright.
Thomas: It makes sense.
Monk: Lots of things make sense, yet we still avoid them. [picks up a small well-worn book and searches through it intently]
Thomas: Oh yeah, makes sense. Eating more fruits and vegetables makes sense. Going to sleep at a reasonable hour makes sense. But we don't always like to do what we know we should do, what we know our God is calling us to do. I'm all too familiar with the difference between common sense and common practice! Sometimes I think I could be the poster-child for it.
Monk: Thomas, we all could be. Father William McNamara, the great mystic of the 20th century said that all the "stuff" of the Church is designed to get you closer to relationship with God. If you can get there without some of that "stuff", go ahead, but I've never met

anyone who could. We need more components than we realize. Even though we like to think we can do without. How did Father McNamara put it…

Thomas: Father McNamara? Are you asking me?

Monk: [Walks over to the old black walnut bookshelf near the woodstove. Looks. Ponders. A lot of indistinguishable muttering. Finally pulls out a small tattered old book] Ahhhh!!! It's in here…. Yes! [Flips through the old book frantically. Points to a page and holds up the book in triumph! Face lights up!] Here it is! Father McNamara said, "Religion is… the way back… to God…. Man's personal encounter with a living God is the ultimate reason for all religious beliefs, duties, obligations, and ceremonies." A personal encounter, Thomas! With the wildness of God, with the living God!

Thomas: The wildness of God! I… What do you do with that? It's… I don't know… It's uncomfortable but at the same time incredibly comforting.

Monk: That's just it. You do nothing with it. You don't have to. I'm not sure you can. Let Him love you! Of course you'll argue that you're not lovable. Good. He's not asking you to be lovable. He's asking you to let Him love you. As you are. He did not make a mistake when He made you.

Thomas: I… What…?

Monk: Be silent. "Be still and know that I am God." Let Him love you. Let. HIM. Love. You!

8. Big Rules and Little Rules

"He who wishes to be perfectly obeyed should give but few orders."
— *St. Filippo Neri*

Thomas: I've been thinking more about all the rules. And what you said about the rules. Pay attention to the big rules, but what about the rest of the rules? All those small rules. Are they unimportant?
Monk: Big or small according to whom?
Thomas: Uh, well, according to your prime directive!
Monk: Ah, some of our conversation is sinking in! But it's not my prime directive.
Thomas: Right. God's. And that's where the little rules come in. Most of the rules really aren't so important.
Monk: Just the opposite. Rules are of paramount importance… that is in relationship to their purpose. The purpose of the rules, which is relationship. Thomas, let's say you start a business. What is the purpose of that business, the prime directive, if you will?
Thomas: Well, to make money. Wait, no! To provide a service. To add value to the people that business serves.
Monk: Okay. Does a business need to make money? Is that a rule?
Thomas: If it wants to stay in business, yes. It can't long fulfill its prime directive if it doesn't make money.
Monk: So the business might have rules about pricing, rules about return policies, rules about hiring, rules about inventory?
Thomas: A lot of rules.
Monk: Some big, some little?
Thomas: Sure.
Monk: And the little rules don't matter?
Thomas: They do, but not as much as the big rules.
Monk: Are you sure?

Thomas: Let's say the business is a restaurant. A little rule might be dress code. Not as important as pricing.
Monk: But inappropriate dress could get in the way of the relationship your restaurant has with its customers. It could even get in the way of the relationship your staff have with each other, yes?
Thomas: I can see that. It reminds me of the great basketball coach, John Wooden. I've read a lot about his approach to coaching and life. You could say he majored on the majors and then majored on the minors within those majors.
Monk: I like that. The sabbath was made for man, not man for the sabbath.
Thomas: What was that about?
Monk: Christ said that to the Pharisees. They always tried to catch him with their rules. No gathering food on the sabbath. You're breaking the rules.
Thomas: And were they? Were they breaking the rules?
Monk: Don't miss the point here! What rule? What is the purpose of the rule?
Thomas: The rule to rest on the sabbath, right?
Monk: But WHY? Why does that rule exist?
Thomas: Isn't it the same reason all the other rules exist? To hold up, support, preserve what you called the right relationship with God and his creation?
Monk: There you go! And I thought you weren't paying attention.
Thomas: Come on now… you don't give me a choice but to pay attention.
Monk: Very funny, Thomas.
Thomas: So there are rules that are more important? And less important rules that can be broken?
Monk: Thomas, do not miss this point. This is of upmost importance.
Thomas: Okay. Tell me how it is!
Monk: Christ says, "The sabbath was made for man, not man for

the sabbath." In other words, the rules are made for man, not man for the rules. Don't make the rules your God. God is God. You can misuse a rule. Remember our conversation about tools?

Thomas: Sure I do. They can be used to create or destroy.

Monk: Rules are tools. The Pharisees were trying to use the rule of obeying the sabbath as a bludgeon. As a weapon to separate people from God. As an instrument of power for themselves. "We know the rules. We are the keepers of the rules. We hold the power." Jesus smacks them upside the head like only He can.

Thomas: Whoah! Does this mean I can – or anyone can – just ignore the rules that we don't want to follow? One of those, "Don't give me you your rules" deals.

Monk: The purpose, Thomas, the purpose!!! Know, love, and serve God in this life. You've heard this? Sound familiar?

Thomas: Vaguely familiar.

Monk: And be happy forever with Him in the next.

Thomas: Right.

Monk: What are you using the rule for? Their purpose is to preserve relationship. To help you to know, love, and serve God. You can misuse them for the opposite end. Remember Jesus warns the people, Do not be hypocrites – who pray in public so that others may see them! He's not saying don't pray. Or even don't pray in public. He's saying that the purpose of your prayer should not be "so that others may see you." It's the same with the sabbath. Rest on the sabbath not so that others may see you, but so that you may build your relationship with your God. Why are you doing it, Thomas? By the way, God didn't rest on the 7th day because He was tired. He rested because He knew you would need a day of rest. He knew we would crowd out time set aside for God. For what matters most.

Thomas: Thank you, Brother, for being patient with me! …at least at times!

Monk: This is why I say, Big or small rules according to whom?

Thomas: If I'm letting a rule get in the way of your – I mean the – prime directive, it's a big deal.
Monk: And if you're ignoring a rule that you need to help you get closer to God, that's also a big deal.
Thomas: Hmmm.
Monk: The parable you know as the Prodigal Son.
Thomas: The son who runs away with all the money?
Monk: That's the one. Jesus doesn't call it the Parable of the Prodigal Son.
Thomas: Okay. So?
Monk: Jesus simply says that a man had two sons.
Thomas: Right. And?
Monk: That's significant because the story, like all of Jesus's parables, is about more than just one person.
Thomas: How is this related to rules?
Monk: Ohhhh… [Deep rich laughter] Well what do you know of the story?
Thomas: The prodigal son runs off and wastes his inheritance…
Monk: Hold on! How did he get that inheritance?
Thomas: I think he asked for it.
Monk: He did. Before his father was dead. That's like wishing your father were dead. Telling your father that his money is more important than his life. Love God and do what you will, indeed!
Thomas: So a rule, don't ask for your inheritance while your father is still alive!
Monk: I think you like rules more than you let on, Thomas. But Saint Francis famously did the same thing.
Thomas: He did?
Monk: In essence, he was spending his inheritance to help rebuild a church, to feed and clothe the poor. To serve God. To feed my sheep! Follow the rule or disobey the rule, but why? The purpose is love of God and love of neighbor.

Thomas: So the prodigal son could have asked for the inheritance to better love God and neighbor?
Monk: Definitely. But then what happens?
Thomas: The son returns and begs forgiveness.
Monk: And the response?
Thomas: The father welcomes him, forgives him. All's well that ends well, eh!
Monk: Is that the whole response?
Thomas: Was there more?
Monk: A man had two sons…
Thomas: Ah, yes! The older brother was so mad. He was not happy. I don't blame him.
Monk: Why don't you blame him?
Thomas: The older brother did everything he was asked to do. He didn't run off. He didn't have any fun.
Monk: He followed the rules?
Thomas: He did!
Monk: Seems you like rules more than you let on.
Thomas: Maybe I do.
Monk: Or maybe you like the rules when you're the one who's been following them. And maybe you, like the older son, are awaiting your reward for following the rules.
Thomas: Or maybe I need to change the subject. I don't like this topic so much anymore. You always seem to hold up a mirror to me.
Monk: Just following the Shepherd's example! Big rules, little rules… the question is, what are you allowing to get between you and God? Whatever you allow to get between you and God… that's a big deal. Let Him love you. And let yourself start to fall in love with Him.

9. Pain, Suffering, Evil and a Loving God?

Thomas: God's perfect. Yet murder, famine, cancer, car accidents, depression, suicide, war, hurricanes, extreme poverty, all exist. More than exist, they happen to some of the best people. Your perfect, loving and all-powerful God allows these things?

Monk: The age-old problem of pain!

Thomas: Couldn't Jesus cure blindness instead of curing one blind man?

Monk: Love and reality collide. You sound angry. This really bothers you?

Thomas: Yes it does.

Monk: Why?

Thomas: It's incongruent. It's inconsistent. God is love. God is perfect. God is all-powerful. Why do so many bad things happen to good people?

Monk: Once again, you're in excellent company.

Thomas: How so?

Monk: Job, Abraham, even Saint Peter – keeper of the keys to the Kingdom, the rock, the first pope – wrestled with God about this.

Thomas: Did they? I'm not letting God off the hook on this one.

Monk: Tell me about the hook.

Thomas: I lost a grandfather before it was his time to go. We never had the chance to say goodbye. He suffered from a massive and sudden heart attack.

Monk: I'm sorry.

Thomas: You don't have to be sorry. You couldn't do anything about it. But God could have.

Monk: You're right.

Thomas: It's not fair. He was a good man. And he was taken before his time.

Monk: Doesn't seem fair.

Thomas: Because it's not. If that's how God operates, I don't like it. I boycott God.

Monk: Thomas, I can see that it bothers you a lot. You want to know why God allows what seems unfair?

Thomas: Not allows. He does it! If God wanted my grandfather to live longer, he's certainly capable of that, isn't he?

Monk: Well…

Thomas: Of course He's capable! Or he's not God! He's capable alright, he just doesn't care. He knows how much pain my family went through, losing my grandfather so suddenly. After his death, my grandmother struggled so much… so much sadness… How could He?

Monk: What would you change, Thomas?

Thomas: Less pain and suffering. Especially for good people. Like my grandmother. She was caught totally off guard when her husband died.

Monk: I can only imagine her sorrow.

Thomas: She was crushed.

Monk: And her story, your story, is repeated so many times across the pages of time.

Thomas: Yeah. And where's God? Perfect, loving, all-powerful God? Fix it.

Monk: Fix it. Get rid of all pain, all suffering?

Thomas: Not all.

Monk: No?

Thomas: No. Just the unnecessary suffering.

Monk: That certainly seems to be a reasonable request.

Thomas: You agree?

Monk: No unnecessary suffering. Yes. I agree.

Thomas: Well then, why does God allow it?

Monk: Maybe He doesn't.

Thomas: Are you saying that He can't stop it?

Monk: Not exactly.
Thomas: Then what are you saying?
Monk: Augustine said that an infinitely good, wise, and powerful God wouldn't allow evil… unless… He could bring an even greater good out of that evil. Your friend Socrates, as he was going to his death, put it this way: "Nothing bad ever happens to a good person, in this life or the next."
Thomas: Socrates said that?
Monk: He did. Let's look at it this way… have you read Tolkien's stories about Hobbits?
Thomas: I have. Great books. The Trilogy of the Ring. The Hobbit.
Monk: Imagine if you ripped a single page out of one of those books, crumpled that page up, allowed that page to be worn out by folding and unfolding, put that page in a bottle and tossed it into the sea. Years later, that bottle washes up on a distant shore and is found by someone who had never heard of the Hobbit. That person takes out the fragment of worn out paper and reads it. Would that reader think that this is an incredible story, one of the greatest stories ever told?
Thomas: Not likely.
Monk: Could that reader wonder about the meaning of that small fragment? Could that reader make presumptions about the character, the story, even about the author?
Thomas: Of course.
Monk: Is it likely that the reader would lack understanding of that page's place in the bigger story?
Thomas: Likely? Well beyond likely! The reader wouldn't have a clue about how that tattered page fit into the bigger story.
Monk: Right.
Thomas: Oh.
Monk: We have to ask, "what is unnecessary?" in the context of the greater story.

Thomas: Hence the reason for the question you keep asking, what would I change.

Monk: And?

Thomas: I'm not sure I have an answer.

Monk: Thomas, over and over people struggled to answer some of Christ's questions. On one famous occasion, Christ asked a group of religious scholars if they would save an ox or one of their own children on the Sabbath, the day of rest. The verse ends with "… they were unable to answer his question."

Thomas: I don't really like that. I want answers.

Monk: You should seek answers. But, my dear Thomas, there is a massive difference between knowing the story and knowing the author.

Thomas: Can I know both? Can I at least strive to know both?

Monk: You can, but which is more important? Knowing all of history or knowing Him?

Thomas: You said that even Peter wrestled with this question.

Monk: He did.

Thomas: How did that go?

Monk: Jesus told his followers that he would suffer and be killed. Peter wrestled with this idea, even arguing with Jesus. Jesus reprimanded Peter, saying, "You are thinking not as God does, but as human beings do." In our example, Peter was thinking like one who has only a tattered page from a 4 volume classic. He wants to change what's written on that page without seeing the rest of the story, or really understanding the author.

Thomas: Who else wrestled with this?

Monk: Who hasn't?

Thomas: You?

Monk: Sure I have. And still do at times. It may be the hardest aspect of God for us to comprehend. He lets us to experience low points in life… pain, struggle, frustration, fear, loneliness, failure, loss. Why? Why??? Thomas, a young elementary school child was once given a caterpillar to take home and care for. The child watched as his caterpillar formed a cocoon. Then the child waited and waited. But, he eventually tired of waiting and cut the cocoon open. Yes, his caterpillar had turned into a butterfly… But that butterfly was never able to fly! You see, the struggle of pushing its wings against the cocoon to break free is precisely what helps the butterfly's wings develop the strength to fly. Our God gives us great clues in nature, if only we'll pay attention!

Thomas: The old "If it doesn't kill ya, it'll make you stronger" argument.

Monk: Clichés stick around for a reason. Some of them contain hints of the truth. You've read Dostoyevsky's Grand Inquisitor?

Thomas: I can't say that I have. You, on the other hand… I'm sure you've read it!

Monk: The Inquisitor challenges Christ about free will, accusing Christ of being evil for allowing mankind the freedom to decide between good and evil. Freedom is a popular idea today, but we need to be careful. Is it *freedom for* or *freedom from*?

Thomas: What do you mean?

Monk: Freedom *for* responsibility or freedom *from* responsibility?

Thomas: Hmmm. Interesting question.

Monk: Which freedom do you worship?

Thomas: Worship?

Monk: Yes, worship. It's not only golden calves that are made into false idols. Ideas can be worshipped as false gods. *Freedom from* is one that has a strong cult following today.

Thomas: Freedom from?

Monk: Yes, freedom from any responsibility. Freedom to do it my way. And have no responsibility for the consequences.

Thomas: And the other option is freedom for?

Monk: Freedom is a tool. Tools, as we discussed earlier, can be used for many purposes. The right purpose or the wrong purpose. Why does God give us so much freedom? What is that freedom for?

Thomas: Choice. Freedom to make choices. Freedom for choosing how we spend our time, how we spend our money, how we treat our neighbors.

Monk: Could you say that freedom is for both making and being responsible for choices?

Thomas: That sounds pretty good.

Monk: Can God be perfect at giving you choices without allowing freedom for you to make choices aligned or not aligned with Him? It's a variation of the classic grade school question, "can God make a rock so big that He can't lift it?"

Thomas: Are you suggesting that bad things, pain, suffering, cancer… have to exist?

Monk: Have to exist is not the same as serving a purpose. Could God make a world without pain and suffering? I would imagine that He could. But would that world serve as a classroom to teach us to love?

Thomas: A classroom to teach us to love?

Monk: How else would you describe it?

Thomas: That's good. I just never heard it before.

Monk: The best classrooms aren't classrooms. And they aren't necessarily easy. How often do we learn to love, learn to forgive, learn to be courageous, develop virtue through adversity? Pain is one of life's greatest clarifiers. It is, as C.S. Lewis said, "Pain is… His megaphone to arouse a deaf world."

Thomas: A deaf world, indeed! Do we need pain to wake us up?

Monk: Remember the story of Jonah? He only reaches out when he's at his lowest, All seems lost when Jonah says, "In my despair, I called out to the Lord."

Thomas: Pain can be good. Nothing bad ever happens to a good person… I may need to wrestle with this on my own for a while.

Monk: You're not alone in that. And you're not alone. Period.

10. God, Why am I Here?

Thomas: What's the point?
Monk: Excuse me?
Thomas: What am I supposed to do with my life? Is there any point to life? I'm lost. I can't believe I'm even saying this out loud. I don't say this to anyone, but sometimes I feel like people can see right through me.
Monk: And what do they see?
Thomas: Everything. And nothing. They can see my doubts, my insecurities, my fears, my hazy confusion, my lack of clarity. No substance. They see it all… and there's not much to see. Forget it.
Monk: I understand. I've been there.
Thomas: You have?
Monk: All too often.
Thomas: You? That's hard to imagine. I don't see that. You come across as so certain. So clear. So convicted.
Monk: So do you.
Thomas: Thanks. But it's a front. It's not real. I'm a fraud.
Monk: No, Thomas.
Thomas: Forget it. I don't know why I'm even telling you this.
Monk: Thomas…
Thomas: No. Let's talk about something else.
Monk: I don't always want to pray.
Thomas: What? Really? You… the monk?
Monk: Really. And it's for those same feelings that you just described.
Thomas: How so?
Monk: Well, not all the time, but when I pray, really pray, I'm putting my whole self before my Maker. And He sees me. All of me.
Thomas: Is He pleased with what He sees?

Monk: That's the question we tend to ask. But it's the wrong question.
Thomas: Wrong?
Monk: Who told me that I wasn't good enough? That I don't have what it takes? Who told you that you weren't good enough? Who told us this? Who told us that we weren't pleasing to our Father?
Thomas: I don't know. Are you asking me?
Monk: I'm asking both of us. Where did this message come from? We all hear it loud and clear. We're no good. We don't have what it takes. We're a disappointment. Who told us this?
Thomas: A parent. Maybe a teacher. A sports coach. Friends. Ourselves. The whole world tells us this, in some way, shape, or form.
Monk: Naked and afraid so they hid! Adam and Eve are the first recorded incident of shame. They hid. Then God shows up. He always shows up. I made you naked. My idea. Ah, you talked to the snake! He made you ashamed of your inadequacy which you don't have...That's the false self, Thomas. We construct this false self. This is who I'm supposed to be. And I'm not. The false self is constantly trying to pay a debt back to its god that it does not owe.
Thomas: Turn on the TV or look at a magazine cover and we see the perfect man or woman. Who we're comparing ourselves to. A lot of influences. A lot of voices.
Monk: Drowning out the one that matters most. The only one who is never disappointed in you.
Thomas: The voice of God? Never disappointed?
Monk: The voice of God. The Infinite. The One who whispers, "Let Me love you! I know all your faults even better than you do. And I love you." That voice. He's crazy about you. And crazy about me. I know... hard to believe. It was hard to believe 2,000 years ago. People in Christ's time didn't think God cared enough to be born in a stable, to live a normal human life, to feel hunger, thirst, abandonment. What sort of God would do that? This was a shock

then and it's still a shock today, 2,000 years later. We've just become immune to the shock.

Thomas: How do we hear that one voice? All the others are so loud, so consistent, so monotonous, so overwhelming.

Monk: Seek that voice.

Thomas: How? It can't be that simple… can it?

Monk: Benedict, around the year 500, left his small village as a young man and journeyed to Rome. He went to study law, but what he found in Rome… it disgusted him. He ran from it. Benedict fled from the noise and moral degradation of Rome to a small town in the mountains, Subiaco. There, in Subiaco, Benedict lived in a cave, in solitude for three years. Three years in a cave! Imagine!

Thomas: What was he running from?

Monk: The noise of the world. We all hide from something. Quite often we hide from the voice of God. Benedict hid from the noise of the world. He grew up believing that Rome would be a city on a hill, a bright light to guide the way. What he found on this first visit was just the opposite. The city was morally corrupt. He sought clarity from the only one who can give it.

Thomas: There. Clarity. Everyone I meet needs more clarity. How do I find clarity?

Monk: Thomas! What are you really asking? What are you *really* asking? It's sort of like the question in John's Gospel, the first question that Jesus asks: "What are you looking for?" In other words, "Why are you asking this? What are you trying to find here? What are you seeking?" That's a central question of our quest.

Thomas: I'm looking for clarity. A purpose. I want to know why I'm here. What I'm supposed to do with my life. In the big areas and the small areas.

Monk: Lots of questions, but they're good ones. Where are you looking for answers? And whose answers are you looking for?

Thomas: You know, Brother, I'm starting to think that monks always answer a question with a question. Is that true?

Monk: Why do you think that?

Thomas: Exactly!

Monk: We all ask a lot of questions. But our God… our God asks at once the toughest and the easiest question of all.

Thomas: What's that?

Monk: God asks, "Will you trust me?"

Thomas: That's it?

Monk: That's a big it, Thomas!

Thomas: Trust is great, but I want clarity.

Monk: You are not the first! Mother Teresa once asked a visiting priest and philosophy professor what she could do for him. The visitor replied: "Please pray for me." Mother Teresa countered with, "What do you want me to pray for?" The man was on sabbatical in India, looking for direction, seeking a purpose for the next phase of his life. He asked her, "Pray that I have clarity." And Mother Teresa, in her wonderfully bold and blunt style… have you ever heard her speak, Thomas?

Thomas: I've heard some of her speeches online. Powerful woman!

Monk: Powerful, indeed! This visiting priest wants her to pray that he will have clarity. She tells him firmly, "No, I will not do that."

Thomas: Seriously? She's something else. But I want clarity.

Monk: Ah, so you're not happy with her answer?

Thomas: No.

Monk: Neither was this priest. He asked for an explanation, and Mother Teresa gave him one! She said, "Clarity is the last thing you are clinging to and must let go of."

Thomas: What kind of an answer is that? I don't like that answer. She had tremendous clarity. How is that fair?

Monk: There you go again, playing God. The priest expressed your exact concern, explaining that she always seemed to have clarity, the clarity he longed for. Mother Teresa laughed and told him, "I have never had clarity. What I have always had is trust. So I will pray that you trust God."

Thomas: So you're giving me the same advice Mother Teresa gave this visiting priest?

Monk: Yes. It's really God's advice. God's voice, asking, "You want clarity? Trust me. I will give you exactly what you need." The problem, Thomas, is this: what you need and what you want are not the same thing. Who knows your deepest, most legitimate needs more? You or God? Who most intimately knows your strengths and weaknesses, your hopes and dreams, your faults and failings? You? Or God?

Thomas: God.

Monk: You seek clarity, but God knows you better than you know yourself.

Thomas: Didn't God give Mother Teresa clarity?

Monk: Certainly. As much as she needed!

Thomas: What does that mean?

Monk: Mother Teresa summed up God's clarity in many ways, but I think this might be the clearest: "At the end of life we will not be judged by how many diplomas we have received, how much money we have made, how many great things we have done. We will be judged by 'I was hungry, and you gave me something to eat, I was naked and you clothed me. I was homeless, and you took me in.'"

Thomas: This is the clarity? I'm supposed to feed the hungry, clothe the naked, shelter the homeless?

Monk: Feed my sheep. Tend my sheep. Christ was abundantly clear about this. Watch Mother Teresa's speech at the National Prayer Breakfast, if you can handle it! She said, "Do not give your leftovers. Give until it hurts."

Thomas: I don't know, Brother. This sounds like too much to ask.

Monk: Sure it does. But God never sends you on a mission without also giving you everything you need for that mission. The problem is not the size of the mission. Remember Adam and Eve in the Garden of Eden?

Thomas: Yes. What about them?

Monk: Well, just that the snake comes and plants the seed of doubt. God made you, but he must have made a mistake. Surely you'll be more perfect, more capable, more god-like if you eat that apple. You're not good enough. God made you, but he didn't give you everything you need. Trust me, not God!

Thomas: Is that the seed of what you called the "False Self?"

Monk: Indeed it is! They eat the apple and, when God comes, they're hiding. Why are they hiding? There's an excellent book called ***Who Told You That You Were Naked?*** by Jacob Raub. One line he has in there seared itself into my memory. "Even in the serial murderer, the image of God cannot be extinguished."

Thomas: We're supposed to see that? We're supposed to find that? The image of God, even in a murderer?

Monk: More importantly, we're supposed to believe it about ourselves. "God doesn't want me. I'm too much of a sinner. This spark of God inside of me, urging me to surrender to mystery, it's obviously not for me!"

Thomas: We're scared of it, I guess?

Monk: Scared to death of it. We're scared to death of what He's going to ask. Jesus in the garden. Ya know? If this can pass, please!

Thomas: Hmm.

Monk: And that's the point where, when you start talking about the things that we're talking about, people try to reduce it to ethics and what do I do, to what's the technique. What they're doing… they're looking for an end run around encounter with God. But they still want to feel good about themselves… feel that they're doing something for their spirituality.

Thomas: Which kind of says it's all or nothing.

Monk: Pardon?

Thomas: It's all or nothing.

Monk: From God's perspective it is. Sure it is. Convincing you of that, okay… Ahh! That's my job.

Thomas: Hahaha! If it's all or nothing, do you give all? You can't!

Monk: Sure you can! Did Jesus give all?

Thomas: He did, yeah. But did He…

Monk: Do you receive a piece of Jesus in the eucharist or do you…

Thomas: But did He resist? Did He resist giving it all? In the Garden of uh…

Monk: Gethsemane.

Thomas: Jesus is saying, "Can we do this some other way?" Right?

Monk: He says, "If this cup can pass from me…" In other words…

Thomas: If there's another way?

Monk: Jesus is true God and true man. One person, but two natures. If He wasn't scared to death at the prospect of going through that horror…

Thomas: Right, then He wasn't true man.

Monk: Then He wasn't human. And He can't answer my fear. That's why we say He nailed our fears to the cross… because He's right there. "Why have you abandoned me?" People must have thought the Apostles were all crazy saying "He's God! He's God!" And then, on the cross, why does He say, "Why have you abandoned me?" Because I say, "Why have you abandoned me?" when the cross comes to my life.

Thomas: Did He feel that?

Monk: Of course He did.

Thomas: Did He feel abandoned by God, even though…

Monk: Of course He did! Why would He lie? But His human nature had to be the cry of Adam on the cross. This fear of abandonment.

Thomas: Which is kind of like my fear of "If I give you everything, it might not work out."

Monk: Hmmmm!

Thomas: Or *my* plan might not work out.

Monk: Hmmm. Yeah. And, of course, you can be sure it's not going to work out if you don't give it over to Him.

Thomas: Right, but you can also be sure it's not going to work out if you do give it over to Him. I mean *your* plans are not going to work out.
Monk: What do you mean?
Thomas: Mary. Mary says, "Okay, you've got it." The angel comes and says, "Mary, I've got a job for you." And she says, "Okay." "Let it be done to me." "Fiat." And then the rest of her life didn't work out probably the way she had planned or hoped.
Monk: No. That's heresy. That's why she was immaculately conceived, without original sin. There was never a moment in her life where she questioned the direction.
Thomas: She never questioned God?
Monk: Matter of fact, one of the most beautiful scenes in Mel Gibson's movie is where she's watching Him being discouraged, and she says to Him, "My son, how will you bring good out of all this?" She doesn't doubt that it's going to happen.
Thomas: She knows.
Monk: She knows. She knows!
Thomas: So when she had to go to Bethlehem, which she probably wouldn't have wanted to do, and when she had to flee to Egypt, and when Joseph died – right? We think Joseph died at some point before Jesus' ministry, right?
Monk: Oh, sure he did.
Thomas: When that happened, since she was without sin, she didn't question God.
Monk: She put it into perspective. Show me Lord, because I know that you're making everything work toward a magnificent end. It's like the Pieta. Mary holding her crucified son. Michelangelo has the best representation. Many of the Pieta have her with tears running down her face, screaming at heaven with her dead son in her arms. With Michelangelo, she's serene, holding her son. Of course, just by the logistics of the marble, she's three times the size of Jesus, but she's holding the dead son. The look on her face… her eyes are

lowered toward Him, not raised in reproach to heaven, but on Him. Because she knows. She's waiting for the first flicker in those eyes of the resurrection that she knows has to happen because this crucifixion happened. Because that was the promise. And God is true to His word. That's the promise of the angel and she…

Thomas: She understood that?

Monk: Oh yes!

Thomas: When she was holding his crucified body?

Monk: Oh yes!

Thomas: Do you think she understood that when He was 2-years-old?

Monk: I think that, just like Jesus…

Thomas: She understood that it was going to be God's plan. Period. And that's it.

Monk: Right. And just like Jesus, she had to grow into an awareness of what it meant to be the Messiah. Don't forget, the wedding feast at Cana… There's a very very funny take on this… A preacher from Tennessee is talking about the wedding feast at Cana. He says, and the essence of this is the southern accent, "And Jesus an' his disciples are sittin' at the taaaable. They're guests at a wedding – a wedding in a smaaaaalll town, not many people, keep that in miiiind, keep thaaat in miiind. They see this couple committin' their liiives as husband as wife for the purposes of God and His covenant and theeeee greatest disgrace… they run outta wiiiiine. No wiiine, no paaarty!" (*back to regular voice*) Now keep this in mind. The coming of the Messiah in Isaiah will be heralded by sweet wine flowing.

Thomas: Oh, really?

Monk: "Son, they have no wiiine. And Jesus turns 'round and says, 'Woman, so what? What's that to me? My hour has not yet come.' Now, they don't record this, but this is what went down between Mary and Jesus. 'Your hour not yet come? The angel told me you the messiah. You were conceived in me by the Holy Spirit to be the messiah. You're 30-years-old. 'Bout time you start to messiiiih!'"

Thomas: Haha ha ha! I love it!

Monk: "And she don't even wait for Jesus to object. She run over to the waiters and say, 'do whatever he tells you. He gonna do somethin'."

Thomas: That's great!

Monk: The thing about the small town of Cana… Thomas, make sure that you know the location. Like if we're describing a very small town in rural New Hampshire. In Cana of Galilee, make sure that you know this is Cana of Galilee.

Thomas: Yeah.

Monk: The probably did textiles there. Very small town.

Thomas: Maybe a hundred people, maybe a few hundred?

Monk: Maybe. Maybe. Probably a couple hundred people were all at the wedding. Maybe a hundred and fifty people. Maybe. And so Jesus goes and makes wine. How much wine does he make? John is very specific.

Thomas: Is it 6… ceramic… not jars… urns?

Monk: Urns, yes. How much each?

Thomas: 10 gallons each, maybe?

Monk: 50 gallons each!

Thomas: Oh!

Monk: 300 gallons of wine.

Thomas: Alright!

Monk: My kind of God.

Thomas: A gallon or two per person at the wedding.

Monk: Only the adults would've been drinking wine.

Thomas: Makes sense.

Monk: Several gallons of wine for each adult. This is my kind of God! That's why I've always said that I believe Jesus was Italian. He changed water into wine because his mother told him to.

Thomas: Ha!

11. Ask the Artist Why

Thomas: You tell me to just trust God. And do whatever I feel like doing?
Monk: Trust, yes. Do whatever you feel like, no. Feelings are a very poor replacement for God! Trust God, not necessarily your feelings.
Thomas: Don't all the psychologists say to trust your feelings?
Monk: No, not all. The good ones understand what feelings are.
Thomas: And what are they?
Monk: A tool. Are emotions to be worshipped? Or are emotions to be observed, sometimes tamed, regulated, respected, ignored, appreciated… depending on the situation?
Thomas: Interesting. Reminds me of Jiminy Cricket in the Disney classic, Pinocchio. Always let your conscience be your guide.
Monk: That's right. Give a little whistle!
Thomas: That cricket doesn't say, "Always let your emotions be your guide!"
Monk: Good thing he doesn't.
Thomas: Pinocchio didn't feel like going to school. He felt like goofing off on Pleasure Island all day long. He felt like chasing easy money and easy fame.
Monk: Some of the traps for one who worships emotions! Surely you've heard the old saying… a finger is good for pointing to the moon, but woe to the man who mistakes the finger for the moon.
Thomas: Surely, I haven't heard that.
Monk: Unfortunately, so many good sayings that capture a glimpse of the truth have disappeared from our vernacular. Like the finger pointing to the moon, emotions point to something. It may be a legitimate fear, or anxiety because we haven't properly prepared for some event. In that case, the emotion is pointing to something we may need to address. Prepare better next time. You're nervous about the test, shut off the electronics and study. Or that's dangerous, use caution. Sometimes, an emotion is a finger pointing right back at

our habits. For example, we don't always feel like getting out of bed in the morning. This could be pointing to many things, for example, poor sleeping habits, a habit of laziness or a lack of passion in our lives.

Thomas: Lack of passion… I can relate. Maybe you know a secret for bringing passion back into everyday life. Isn't it linked to clarity? To knowing what I'm supposed to do with my life? Where do I get this passion?

Monk: Pray.

Thomas: I do, now and then.

Monk: Excellent. Pray more.

Thomas: Pray? That's it? Is that all you've got?

Monk: I would start there. Consult the designer. How's your prayer life?

Thomas: Oh boy. It's… well…

Monk: Deep, meaningful, personal, consistent?

Thomas: Not the words I'd probably use.

Monk: That's why I recommend starting there. Talk with the Designer. What's the purpose of the creation? Talk with the Creator. Ask.

Thomas: Ask? How do I do that?

Monk: Like that.

Thomas: Like what?

Monk: Like you just did. Ask a question. Talk *with* God instead of talking to, at, or about God. It seems we all like talking to or about God without talking with Him. Talking *with* constitutes listening, not just talking. Try a simple question. "God, what do you want me to do here?" or "God, what do you want me to notice, pay attention to, hear, think about?"

Thomas: Right. Then what?

Monk: Then listen. What do you normally do when you ask a question? Oh, wait!!! I know that answer. You like to ask a second question before getting the first answer!

Thomas: Guilty as charged! I can't argue that one, Brother.

Monk: Oh, I think you could.

Thomas: Ask a question and then listen. This is praying?

Monk: Of course. Have you ever taken one of those art appreciation courses?

Thomas: Sure. Several. Even some of my Lit courses in college felt like an art appreciation course.

Monk: Why do you say that?

Thomas: The professor kept telling us what the author meant by certain parts. How would the prof know the author's intent?

Monk: Exactly! What the artist had in mind… It's often just a guess. Perhaps an educated guess, but still a guess. But, what if you could ask the artist?

Thomas: That's what I'm talking about!

Monk: So am I! Ask the Artist about His masterpiece, you.

Thomas: Masterpiece. Sure. Not sure I always feel like a masterpiece.

Monk: Don't go back to worshipping feelings. Everything the Master touches is a masterpiece.

Thomas: I'm still not so sure on this idea of asking God what He wants me to do and then just waiting for an answer.

Monk: That's not the only approach.

Thomas: What else do you recommend?

Monk: Are you the only person who sought clarity?

Thomas: Of course not. I imagine that almost everyone since the beginning of time has wanted clarity.

Monk: Do you think any of them asked God for clarity?

Thomas: Sure.

Monk: Did He answer them?

Thomas: I don't know.

Monk: How would you find out?

Thomas: Ahhhh…

Monk: Maybe some of those quests are written down somewhere?

Thomas: You're suggesting that I read the Bible?

Monk: It is the owner's manual. The artist's journal. If the consummate engineer designed us, wouldn't you want to read His book to figure out what you're supposed to do?

Thomas: Makes a lot of sense.

Monk: Glad to hear it. When will you begin?

Thomas: Are you suggesting that I read the owner's manual from cover to cover?

Monk: No. Start with one of the Gospels. Spend time with Christ. Get to know his voice. Did He always have clarity? What did He do to better understand His mission? Did people ask Him for guidance? How did he guide them? As you read, pray. Ask Him to show you the relevance of what you're reading to your current situation.

Thomas: You've done this?

Monk: Still do. There really is no arriving. When you arrive, you're no longer here!

Thomas: And He speaks to you through this journey?

Monk: Thomas, the Gospel is not merely a history of events that happened. The Gospel describes events that both happened and continue to happen in our world. Get to know one of the Gospels. Listen to Christ's voice. He promised, "My sheep listen to my voice."

Thomas: I'm not sure I make a good sheep!

Monk: Thomas, you spend a lot of time working in the leadership space. You've quoted leaders, entrepreneurs, people who change the world. Can I ask, who was the greatest leader in all of history?

Thomas: All of history? Can we just look at the last hundred years? Even then, that's a tough question. How would you quantify "greatest"?

Monk: You decide. Much of your career deals with this, yes?

Thomas: It does. Hmmm. Great leader could probably be quantified by something along the lines of "lasting positive impact".

Monk: Okay.

Thomas: If that's our measurement, there are some names that come to mind but…

Monk: But?

Thomas: But, I know who you're trying to get me to say!

Monk: Is that so? I have an agenda?

Thomas: It has to be Jesus. Whether you think He is God or not, His lasting positive impact on the world is beyond comparison. There's not really even a close second.

Monk: Is that so?

Thomas: No one close. Even most of those who might have been on my list were massively influenced by Jesus. From MLK to Gandhi to the founder of Habitat for Humanity.

Monk: Interesting. And how well do you know this greatest leader in all history? His story? His life? His communication style? His decisions? His questions?

Thomas: Not so well.

Monk: Thomas, He has plans for you. Those plans are more incredible than any plans you'll come up with on your own. Get to know the Shepherd!

Thomas: You know, I spotted an old dusty Bible on the book shelf in this cabin. I might just take you up on that challenge.

Monk: You won't regret it. I've never met someone who regretted reading the Bible. But beware. It's dangerous to the false self!

12. Trust… even without Clarity!

Thomas: I started to read through one of the Gospels.
Monk: Really? You're reading the Bible? Excellent! You won't be disappointed. It will challenge, convict, inspire, and encourage you.
Thomas: Much to my surprise, yes, it already is doing those things and I'm only about 10 pages into one Gospel. What next?
Monk: Thomas! You keep wanting step 1, 2, 3. NO!!! You want a predictable God, a God you can control. That's no god at all. You want Him to behave the way you think He should behave. Let God be God!
Thomas: No more advice, then? To have more clarity, you recommended prayer and reading the Bible. That's all you've got?
Monk: What are you really looking for? A cookie-cutter god? Thomas, you can't pre-empt the Holy Spirit. You and I don't get to decide how it develops. It's never the same. If you're really looking for God, you'll find Him. If you're really looking for His plans for your life, you'll find them. But it won't happen the way you expect, I'll guarantee you that! You'll be driving in the car, mowing the lawn, sitting on a park bench… when BAM! All of a sudden you have an Aha moment. Okay? You don't get to decide how or when.
Thomas: God's not predictable, eh?
Monk: You can say that again! Si comprehendis, non est Deus.
Thomas: What's that? Si comprehendis…
Monk: …non est Deus. Augustine. If you understand it is not God. If we comprehend something, completely understand it, can predict it, it's not God we're talking about! And God is certainly not predictable. Never been my experience!
Thomas: Can you tell me more about your experience?
Monk: Many years ago, when I was in my teens and twenties, I too was seeking clarity. Desperately. I found… no. That's wrong. He… He – God – immersed my life in the lives of the saints. Each saint

that I encountered, I slowly began to see that there is one area where they all, all of the saints, seemed to have clarity.

Thomas: There is?

Monk: Yes. They all asked what Christ demanded of them in each moment. In their own unique ways, of course.

Thomas: That's great, but I'm not convinced it's all that helpful.

Monk: Put it another way. Ask yourself, what does love demand of me in this moment?

Thomas: God is love. Love is God. And love is all you need!

Monk: Nice singing, but not exactly. God is love, yes, but God is also much more than just love. Love alone does not define God. God is also truth, justice, wisdom, art, beauty.

Thomas: Okay, okay! It was just an expression.

Monk: Carelessness with language, naturally including sayings that are "just expressions" can lead us down the wrong path.

Thomas: Oh, I think I understand how you feel about that by now! Back to trust and clarity. I'm looking for clarity, and you're telling me to trust, and ask what love demands of me in this moment?

Monk: It's like when the woman says to Jesus, "Blessed is the womb that bore you. Blessed are the breasts that nursed you." Jesus says Oh no. No, no, NO! I'm not letting you off the hook like that. She's not blessed because of her breasts and womb. She's not blessed because she's my mother. That lets you off the hook. You can't be my mother and so you're not called to the same holiness?

Thomas: Oh wow. That's uncomfortable.

Monk: She's blessed because she heard the word of God and kept it. She sought the will of God and she kept it. And that's where you become the womb, my mother and brothers and sisters.

Thomas: Is this like when Mother Teresa would tell people to find their own Calcutta? She used to tell people who would visit her, "This is not your Calcutta. Yours is somewhere else."

Monk: Great example! I didn't know that she used to say that.

Thomas: Brother, I read about a nun in Buffalo, New York, who went to visit Mother Teresa. She told Mother Teresa that she wanted to join her. Mother Teresa wrote her a letter essentially saying thank you, but no thanks. Your Calcutta is not here. Mother Teresa told this nun and many other people, "Find your own Calcutta."

Monk: Right.

Thomas: I'm not sure we're making progress here.

Monk: Is that the goal, progress?

Thomas: I think so.

Monk: I don't.

Thomas: Well then, what do you think the goal is?

Monk: Answering your quest. Which is the quest of all of humanity. I met Mother Teresa once. It was brief, but that encounter is seared into my memory.

Thomas: You really met her?

Monk: I did. It was San Francisco in 19… 82. She was there to celebrate the 800th birthday of Saint Francis and Mother was speaking at a gorgeous old cathedral. The place was packed. Overflowing with people. Standing room only. Bishops, Cardinals, all decked out. Powerful people, politicians, business people. Mother Teresa started to speak, all five feet nothing of her, maybe 90 pounds… She's barely tall enough to be seen over the podium. Oh, but she started speaking and that place fell utterly silent. You could hear a pin drop. The holiness of that woman, the truth, the conviction, the spirit… she commanded attention.

Thomas: What did she say?

Monk: Her words spoke directly into our souls.

Thomas: A soul on fire. Setting the world on fire.

Monk: Ahh! The words of Catherine of Siena. I'm impressed. When Mother Teresa finished speaking, the round of applause was thunderous. As she made her way through the crowd, she suddenly turned and veered off her path, heading directly toward me. I was standing in the back and had been praying about a very difficult situation, a decision that was weighing heavily on my heart. Mother

Teresa walks directly towards me and the crowd parts to allow her through. She walked up to me, put her hand on me and, with that indescribable intensity, stared into my eyes. She said, “You must do what God wants!” Then she simply turned and walked away. Just like that, she was gone. A soul on fire, indeed!

Thomas: Incredible.

Monk: It was. Still is. It was decades ago and I still remember it like it was this afternoon. Thomas, that’s your answer.

Thomas: Do what God wants? But I don’t know what that is. How would I know…

Monk: Sure you do.

Thomas: I do? I don’t think so.

Monk: Yes, you do. In some area of your life, it is abundantly clear.

Thomas: I’m not seeing it, Brother.

Monk: Do you want to see it?

Thomas: Yes.

Monk: Are you sure?

Thomas: I am sure.

Monk: Then you’ll see it. He promised that. Seek and you shall find. But you must seek.

Thomas: Seek what?

Monk: God’s will. What does love demand of you in everyday life situations?

Thomas: It’s that simple?

Monk: The concept is simple. Execution might not be as simple.

Thomas: It’s not exactly the answer I was looking for.

Monk: Benedict says, “He should only be admitted to the monastery who truly seeks God.” The only criteria. Simple. Doesn’t need a resume or letter of recommendation. Does he truly seek God? Because then we can do that together and do something beautiful for God, so to speak. Make something wonderous happen. What are you seeking? What are you looking for? The questions we’ve been asking throughout our time together.

Thomas: If I want to do what God wants me to do, He'll show me? He'll guide me? I'll find Him and my purpose?
Monk: His purpose for you.
Thomas: Right.
Monk: Christ prays in the garden, "Thy will be done." Over and over, He says, "Follow me."
Thomas: Follow Him where? How?
Monk: To the cross.
Thomas: That's unreasonable.
Monk: He's unreasonable. You want a reasonable God, sorry. That's not the God we got.
Thomas: But follow Him to the cross?
Monk: He says it. Take up your cross.
Thomas: What's the practical application of this? I give up my life?
Monk: You're giving up your will to follow His. You're in a meeting at work. Somebody is late. You feel like being obnoxious, giving that person a rude look. Making a comment. His will, your cross, is giving up what you want to do or say in that moment. Asking, "What does love demand of me in this moment?" Seeing that person as Christ sees that person. Christ even challenges us to see that person as Christ, himself.
Thomas: So you're saying be nice to the person who walked in late to the meeting?
Monk: Nice? No, Thomas! Was Christ always nice?
Thomas: Wasn't He? He wasn't always kind? I thought He was.
Monk: Thomas, He was always Christ.
Thomas: Like that bumper sticker! Have you ever seen it?
Monk: Which one?
Thomas: It says, "What would Jesus do? Remember that flipping over tables and chasing people with a whip are among the options."
Monk: I haven't seen that one but I like it. He was always Christ!
Thomas: So it doesn't always mean just being kind?
Monk: He said, "Follow me." He's still saying, "Follow me."

Thomas: Follow me is akin to asking, "What does love demand of me in this moment?"
Monk: Yes. Sometimes it's listening. Other times, it's questioning, or teaching. Aquinas said that the greatest charity we can do for another is to lead them to the truth. That's not always convenient. That's your flipping over tables bumper sticker. Christ is the Truth. Chesterton so brilliantly said he didn't need the church to tell him he was wrong when he knew he was wrong. He needed the church to tell him he was wrong when he thought he was right!
Thomas: Ouch! What does love demand of me is starting to sound a lot tougher than I thought.
Monk: Certainly. And it evolves. It's never the same. That's why I live in New England. I would have chosen to live here no matter what. The mountains, the rivers, the lakes. But we are very capable of becoming immune to the beauty, to God's fingerprints. We need to choose to see. Practice seeing.
Thomas: But it seems like a lot of the awe – that awe of seeing something for the first time – fades. Or it's numbed.
Monk: That's why you have to see something with new eyes.
Thomas: Makes sense.
Monk: Once you fall in love with someone, does your vision of that person ever fade?
Thomas: No. Well, it can fade.
Monk: You're looking for your wife in the airport. Seeing her face. That feeling. Is it any different than the first time you saw her? That's why we insist so much on allowing oneself to see what God sees. Metanoia. The word has been used and misused from the dawn of Christianity, variously translated as "conversion", "a turn-about" a process of change, "coming to one's senses" among other concepts. Metanoia literally means "beyond thought", acquiring a whole new way of thinking, believing, perceiving far beyond one's hitherto conditioned – and sometimes entrenched – thoughts, beliefs and perceptions. It has too often been robbed of its awesome power.

In short, metanoia is to "put on the mind of Christ" as Paul exhorts the early Church at Philippi.

Thomas: Powerful. I need some of that. Is there a way to nurture that - metanoia?

Monk: Don't let your heart become drowsy from the anxieties of daily life. If you let it, your heart will become drowsy.

Thomas: But how? How do you avoid becoming drowsy from daily routines?

Monk: By deliberately seeing. Which is what contemplation is. Taking time to let nothing else get in the way of your seeing.

Thomas: Deliberate.

Monk: Knowing that you're not going to see or hear anything. Total availability to whatever God wants to do. That day. Because it's never the same.

Thomas: What you're saying about the pursuit of clarity is very different than what I expected.

Monk: Hmmm.

Thomas: It's very different from what I hear from the rest of the world.

Monk: And?

Thomas: And… I like it. It carries a weight, a depth. It's not as straightforward as I had hoped, but I'm starting to think that it isn't supposed to be.

Monk: Unless you become like children… you will not enter the kingdom of heaven. Childlike awe. Humility. Wonder.

Thomas: Awe! There it is again. Little children see the world with a sense of wonder, full of awe for the mystery of it all.

Monk: Thomas, if you ever study one of the martial arts, there is an intriguing concept. To a beginner, a punch is just a punch. Then it becomes more than a punch. Finally, it becomes just a punch again.

Thomas: What? What does that mean?

Monk: What do you think it means?

Thomas: A beginner just sees a punch as a punch. Then, with some learning, the punch becomes more. Different punching styles, each with a lot of fundamentals. How the body turns, the best way to make a fist, how to focus, arm angle, timing… a lot of details. It becomes complicated. The punch is more than a punch. Then, with mastery, the punch just becomes a punch again. All the complexity is still in there, but it doesn't need to be explained. It doesn't demand the same attention.

Monk: Very good. And? How does this relate to God, purpose, awe? Or does it?

Thomas: Becoming like children would be going back to seeing God as something so indescribable, so full of mystery, so full of wonder. God becomes complicated when we are working through all the details. Why would He send His son? How are we supposed to live our lives? What did Christ mean when He said… just about anything... Then, God becomes just God… I can't use that expression, but God becomes something so incredible, so wonderous, that words can't come close to describing.

Monk: I think you're on to something. Thomas Aquinas, one of the most brilliant minds ever to walk the earth, wrote millions of words in his lifetime. The equivalent of about 500 modern books! Nearing the end of his life, Aquinas said that all his writing was nothing but straw! Straw, Thomas! Good for what? Lining the stalls of the pigs.

Thomas: Maybe he was just having a moment of self-doubt.

Monk: Ridiculous! Aquinas, just a few months before his death, had a vision. Christ said to him, "You have written well of me, Thomas; what reward will you have?" Thomas replied, "Only yourself, Lord." Aquinas stopped writing after that. He put down his pen.

Thomas: Incredible! He wrote that much only do decide that no words could really describe God?

Monk: Exactly! Keep in mind – and I love the irony here – Aquinas was born just a year before Francis of Assisi's shining life on earth came to an end.

Thomas: Okay. And?
Monk: Francis lived his life as if a punch were just a punch. God was an incredible mystery. Francis didn't need to try to put God into words. Aquinas spent much of his waking hours trying to put God into words before finally realizing that words about God were mere straw compared with an encounter with the living God! The wildness of God!
Thomas: Are you saying that we shouldn't even try to understand God? Or think about the tough questions?
Monk: Not at all. What I'm saying is that even the most brilliant minds, if they stay humble, eventually step back in a childlike – not childish, mind you – child-*like* awe and utter a deep and profound "Wow!"
Thomas: Can you connect all of this back to my purpose?
Monk: I think that *you* can. Care to give it a shot?
Thomas: Hmmm. The punch thing, asking "what does love demand of me?", finding ways to keep the awe alive… It all goes back to, "Let God be God." Let Him guide you as much or little as He will. Look for Him and His will in your journey.
Monk: Thomas, that's pretty good. But…
Thomas: Aw, come on! Can't it just be pretty good without the but?
Monk: This *but* is an important *but*. It's about your intimate relationship with your Creator. All the good deeds you think you're supposed to do… Why do good things? Why encourage or challenge others? Why forgive? Why? Because you allow yourself to experience the wildness of God, which in turn gives you a glimpse of the wildness of His image in you. Which you absolutely need to share. Do you love me? Feed my sheep. Do you love me? Tend my sheep. Do you love me? Feed my lambs. The reason we ask these big questions, the reason we feel unsettled more often than not… we're just not satisfied with where we are with God. And we can't be. There is no…

Thomas: We're supposed to be unsettled? Can't get no satisfaction, is that it? That's how God set it up?
Monk: Thomas, you don't need constant conversion if you're satisfied. That's why I keep going back to the question, "Are you satisfied with your relationship with God?"
Thomas: Do you ask that question… of yourself?
Monk: I'm a monk. The Psalms ask it for me every morning.
Thomas: So, you ask it every day. And the answer is never "Yes"?
Monk: No. The answer is, "Here's where we're going. Get on board or get off."
Thomas: The answer is what you called constant conversion?
Monk: The answer is: "Trust Me!" Yes. Constant. Metanoia.
Thomas: And every day you're not as trusting as you could be?
Monk: No, I didn't say that. The whole point of my being there is because I trust Him. The point is, what He asked me to trust Him for yesterday is not what He's asking me to trust Him for today.
Thomas: Compare that to the Virgin Mary, as you were talking about earlier. She never responded with a "Huh, I don't know about this plan."
Monk: No. Well, that is the attitude. That's why we end all our prayers to God with a prayer to the Virgin Mary. "Give me a double portion of your spirit." So that whatever is coming my way, I trust that this is somehow for my salvation or for the salvation of another. But, in any case, it's what God's will is for me here. And part of my surrender to the mystery is this trusting that even the things that hurt me the most and annoy me the most are somehow in service to the Kingdom.
Thomas: Is that the point of life?
Monk: Huh?
Thomas: Is that the point of life, to be of service to the Kingdom?
Monk: No. The point of life is completeness in God, is wholeness in God. Part of the journey involves all of those criteria. But again, it's not a journey that you take in one step… you take halting steps.

You can take steps backwards. You can limp at times. Or stumble.

Thomas: I had the chance to give the keynote at a high school graduation two summers ago and one of the biggest points I tried to make was that everybody in the world is going to ask these kids, "What do you want to do? Where do you want to go? What do you want to study?" They'll ask lots of "what do *you* want?" questions. That might be the wrong question.

Monk: Hmmm.

Thomas: Kids constantly ask, and I think adults, too. We constantly ask, "What's the point? What's the purpose? Why am I here? What am I doing here? What am I supposed to do?" Trying to find myself questions. Years ago, I read a lot of books about purpose, finding your purpose, finding your mission, your why. Figure out why you're here and then get to work on the how.

Monk: *Your* why. A self-defined why. And by definition, a self-parametered why.

Thomas: Yes.

Monk: If you were going to decide, that's the *False Self.*

Thomas: Right. That's what it felt like.

Monk: These are the possibilities. This is your *Why*. How do you know? Did you consult the Source of the why? The ultimate Asker of the question? Thomas, we all ask these questions because God created us with a homing device, so to speak.

Thomas: Then how does a young person… maybe this goes back to Augustine's "our heart is restless until it rests in You." Are we supposed to help people find their Why? Not *their* Why, but His why for them?

Monk: Not from that part of the quote… because you forgot the first part. Augustine said, "*You* made us for *Yourself*, oh Lord, and our heart is restless until it rests in You." That's to seek. Not to find the source of the restlessness. To find the source of me. "You made us for Yourself." That's why I'm restless. That's why I'm haunted.

I think haunted is a much better translation of that from the rhetorical Latin of Augustine.

Thomas: "Our heart is haunted…"

Monk: Haunted, yeah.

Thomas: Haunted. Even hunted, maybe?

Monk: Haunted by "Is this all there is?" Certainly you've seen athletes who have won it all, yet the haunting remains. The whisper of "Is this all there is?" I recall seeing an interview where Tom Brady, with all his fame, wealth, and popularity, used almost these exact words after winning yet another Superbowl. Brady's facial expression, his body language, his whole being betrayed him in that interview. He finally admitted that he wasn't as happy winning the Superbowl as he thought he'd be. He fumbles with the answer before finally admitting, "There's got to be more than this."

Thomas: Really?

Monk: Oh yes. Really.

Thomas: I have to look up that interview. Hard to believe.

Monk: Why is it hard to believe?

Thomas: Well, Brady has what everyone wants.

Monk: Does he?

Thomas: Sure.

Monk: Surely not. Watch the interview.

Thomas: I will.

Monk: Haunted. That's what you'll see. Restlessness.

Thomas: If that's Tom Brady, what hope is there for the rest of us?

Monk: Hope? More than hope. It's a promise. Seek and you'll find. Seek God's purpose for your life. Most of us ask God to help us find our own purpose. Change the prayer. Ask your God to help you see what He has in mind for you. Augustine answered the question. "You have made us for Yourself!" And that's WHY our heart is restless until it rests in Him!

13. Pray? Why? How? For What?

Thomas: People pray. Some pray an awful lot! Or at least they like to say things like, "I'll pray for you." Brother, what happens when people pray? Are prayers really answered? Everyone says that they pray, but it seems that most prayers are just a grocery list for God. God, could you do this for me and this, and while you're at it, could you straighten out my in-laws?

Monk: And God always answers prayer. You can't even say the word prayer unless the Holy Spirit stirs it up. You can't pray unless the Spirit of God brings it to your lips. And the Spirit brings it to Jesus. Then Jesus takes it and He pleads it before the Father.

Thomas: So when I'm praying, I'm not really praying?

Monk: Of course you are.

Thomas: But you just said that I can't pray unless the Spirit of God brings the words to my lips.

Monk: Thomas, we've been through this before. Free will! You can ignore, you can resist, you can go against the nudges from the Spirit. I'm quite certain that you have plenty of experience with this!

Thomas: Wow. There you go… I'm a sinner! Guilty.

Monk: As am I. I say this because we all have plenty of experience with ignoring the voice of God. To our own peril, of course, but we do it, nonetheless.

Thomas: I can't argue with that, Brother!

Monk: Do you imagine that the Spirit of God, with His Son in whose name He refuses nothing, asks Him and God says, "No"? No! God says, "Wait a minute. I have a better idea for what you want. I have a better idea of what you're asking than you do. Sometime… not now… but stay tuned." But He never says, "No." God never says "No" to prayer. God always answers prayer.

Thomas: Let's say I'm praying for one of my kids, one of my children. Let's say that my daughter is going through a rough time and I'm praying for her.

Monk: Thomas, why are you praying for your child? [Pause] Because you love your child?
Thomas: Yes.
Monk: That's what He's answering. "I know what you want… for her. You… use these words. But what you really want is this. And I'm going to give it to you." So it turns out very very different from what you think.
Thomas: Wow.
Monk: Yeah, wow.
Thomas: Even when a parent is praying for… this is tough. I spoke at a conference and Jim Kelly was one of the speakers. Jim Kelly was a quarterback for the Buffalo Bills…
Monk: Yes, I know.
Thomas: He lost his child. 8-year-old kid. Cystic Fibrosis.
Monk: Cystic Fibrosis. Horrible.
Thomas: Eight-years-old... I imagine he was praying like crazy. I didn't know that side of his story. He spoke about losing four Super Bowls in a row and then described it as preparation. Preparation to get him ready for a real loss.
Monk: Hmmm.
Thomas: He had to be praying for his kid to be better, right? And God did what?
Monk: I think he was praying for God's mercy for the child.
Thomas: Oh.
Monk: Thomas, years ago, a woman I had known since she was a child got married and she conceived twins. Everything was fine… but… Around the third month of her pregnancy, she got an infection. The twins were born at 1 pound 5 ounces and 1 pound 7 ounces. Blind.
Thomas: Ohhh!
Monk: And I was… I was… on my knees constantly. And when it looked… when it finally came to… this went on for 8 weeks… They

tried to save these kids. Tried to operate… There was just… Don't forget they were twins and born at five and a half months.

Thomas: Oh boy.

Monk: The doctors tried mightily to save them. And when it finally came to the point where it was obvious that they were not going to survive, because God knows what our medical capabilities are, I was so angry. So I went to the Blessed Mother with my anger. And right in the middle of it, she smacked me right upside the head. "Do you think that you love these children more than I do?"

Thomas: Hmmm.

Monk: You're praying for their best. And *this*… This *is* their best.

Thomas: This is their best.

Monk: God doesn't cause disease. God doesn't cause death. But He allows it as a mercy. The way we've messed up the world… If we weren't spending billions on bombs, we would have found a way to save these children, a way to alleviate that infection. We don't do God's will and then we come back and yell at Him! He's merciless?

Thomas: Hmmm. So I pray, we pray, but God… maybe translates our prayers?

Monk: He knows you better than you know yourself. He knows our limits. He knows our pains. He knows. And He listens. And He answers. But, more importantly, He is with us. Emmanuel means "God with us."

Thomas: So when we pray, God is with us?

Monk: Always. His promise, "I am with you always." And our God… oh, Thomas! Our God keeps His promises.

Thomas: So I pray, God is with me, God hears my prayers, but then He does what He wants with them?

Monk: Let God be God, Thomas. God never thinks He's you, but you, on the other hand…

Thomas: I know, I know. I like thinking, "If I were God, I'd…"

Monk: Dangerous territory.

Thomas: Thinking?

Monk: No. Thinking is using the incredible mind that God gave you. Comparing ourselves to God, wanting to control God, *that* is the dangerous territory.

Thomas: History repeats itself, eh? It's been said that the only thing we learn from history is that we don't learn from history.

Monk: Clever. Remember Jacob wrestling with God?

Thomas: Oh yeah. How could I forget that?

Monk: God renamed him Israel, "One who wrestles with God."

Thomas: Yes, you told me that.

Monk: God is the only one who can give us a new name. He gives us our identity, so He, alone, can give us a new identity.

Thomas: Intriguing! But it makes sense.

Monk: At the end of a long night wrestling with God, Jacob's hip was dislocated. The Bible tells us that Jacob limped away because of his injured hip. Jacob – Israel – never took another sure step for the rest of his life. From that day on, he walked with a limp. Unsure. Humble. When we encounter the Living God, we walk away humbled. Not humiliated, as the culture and the great deceiver might lead you to believe. No. But humbled, yes!

Thomas: Humbled. With a limp.

Monk: Knowing that there are things that we just don't comprehend. There are reasons beyond the grasp of our finite minds.

Thomas: And this is why we pray, but God does what He chooses?

Monk: God is God. But that does not mean that He doesn't hear us or care about what we care about. His understanding is beyond ours.

Thomas: How should I pray, then?

Monk: Good question. You do know that the Apostles asked Christ that exact question?

Thomas: Sure. The Lord's Prayer.

Monk: And, in that prayer is your answer.

Thomas: I should say the "Our Father"?

Monk: Sure. But not just say. Pray.

Thomas: Okay.
Monk: Part of the prayer is "Thy will be done."
Thomas: So just pray that God gets what He wants?
Monk: Thomas, Thomas, Thomas! Prayer flows from, a priori, your grounding in God. When you go into contemplation, you can't go there as Thomas. You can't go there as a husband or father. You gotta go there as the man God created that somebody gave the name Thomas to. But when you come out of contemplation, you go back to the husbandry and fatherhood and all those kinds of things with a whole different perspective, for this specific issue for this day. That's why contemplation is an ongoing process. It not only immerses you, but it immerses all those loves that God has willed in your life, into this swirling perfection. Little by little, more and more. Which is why Karl Rahner says that the prime demand of your baptism is contemplation. It's…
Thomas: Who's Karl Rahner?
Monk: You can look him up. You're not getting us off track this time! The first word of the rule of Saint Benedict, the rule of seekers… the first word is "Listen." Listen! And don't listen with ears for what you want to hear. Don't listen as any of the things I described: Thomas the husband, father, business person. Listen for… your mind has to be completely free, all the distractions that flowed in flow right out. You neither resist them – in which case you're never going to get rid of them… don't think of a yellow monkey. Do not think of a yellow monkey! Do not resist them and don't embrace them. It's like a bird passing though the sky. It doesn't leave a tear in the sky when it flies through. Let it go on its way. So, the field is cleared again. The word contemplation comes from the preface of the Roman priests, Pagan priests. The Roman forum was built in square form and at the Temple of Jupiter, the people would come and ask them for an Oracle. They'd ask them to read the signs. The *Templa* was that space in the sky that was defined by the tops of buildings, and the priests would sit there with

no thought in their mind, not even the question the person asked, and they'd wait for the Augurs, for the birds to fly over or the clouds to reveal something… and then they would have their answer. Their interpretation. But they would have their answer. To the Christian, it's the same thing. God… we *know* He's there! We *know* that we exist because of Him. And that He exists not only there, but here [hand to temple and then on heart]. And that the God within and the God without constantly seek to be in a swirling communication, constantly changing the water, so to speak, for the newest circumstances, the newest thoughts, the newest temptations, whatever the circumstances are. To allow that – is contemplation! but you can't go in there as… I can't go in there as monk!

Thomas: Right.

Monk: Because then I expect God to say monk things to me. Okay? And God doesn't want to deal with the monk today. God wants to deal with the cancer patient today. You know?

Thomas: I think I'm starting to.

Monk: And I will have nothing to say to a cancer patient I may meet next week if I refuse to be the cancer patient today. Because that's the only reason that I believe all this is happening. And I didn't realize it till I went through my second chemo. I watched my mother die of cancer. I watched her go through chemo. I watched her lose her hair. I watched her fade down to 78 pounds, in front of my eyes. I went home for 18 months and watched my mother die. Okay, still, I had no idea what she was going through.

Thomas: Yeah.

Monk: Now, I pass by all those people in hospital rooms. I look into their eyes and I see. Compassion means *to suffer with*, and when you *suffer with* them, Christ suffers with them. It gives meaning to the suffering. It doesn't pity. It means to suffer with, that you are suffering with them as Christ is suffering with them. And it's a whole different thing. *Whole different thing!* Because now I know. Now I know what I have to say when their questions come up.

Thomas: Right. So, everything has meaning then, related to know, love, and serve God?

Monk: Everything. Everything.

Thomas: But it's always related to know, love, and serve God?

Monk: Yes.

Thomas: And others, then?

Monk: Right. Or avoiding. Not doing those things. Yeah.

Thomas: So, everything in your life helps you to be better at loving God and others.

Monk: The contemplative sees bubbles in the water and sees God creating the world.

Thomas: Uh huh.

Monk: Everything in creation is meant to speak to it. This is the great gift of the eyes of Francis. Of course, almost 800 years before Francis, Benedict has a vision just before his death of everything in the world coming together in a single beam. And the beam was transfigured by purpose, it says in the Latin text of Saint Gregory. The word for purpose is the same word that's used for inspiration, in other words, the spirit being shot through it, in other words, everything in the world. Like I said with the beginning of the prayer over the chalice. What it really means is you restore our eyes to see the beauty of your transforming presence that is available to me as a transforming presence, if I only see. And that's what it is for me. And I surrender to that. Try telling God it's only a flower opening. I'm sorry, it is not!

Thomas: It's the transforming presence of God!

Monk: And that's why solitude. That's why quiet. That's why monks built monasteries and, for centuries, seekers from all walks of life and from all corners of the globe went to these monasteries. The monastery, a dedicated space of beauty and solitude, is a valuable catalyst in this process, because look at all the contrivances we have around… distractions, entertainments, toys, devices, the things that we've come to depend upon.

Thomas: But people don't do it, though! They don't go to the quiet places! They don't pray in silence. I mean, even when they know it changes them, people…

Monk: Thomas! They don't know! They would not be able to resist it if they knew! If only they could taste for one moment… If only they could taste for one moment what this means! And God does give those moments to everybody, they're called peak moments.

Thomas: We all have those.

Monk: Driving along, out of the blue, all of sudden…

Thomas: That's a taste of one of those moments. And then we still resist! That's what I'm saying.

Monk: But we don't resist. We can't hold on to it because we have nowhere to go with it. We hate when the peak moment starts to pass.

Thomas: Sure.

Monk: …and we try to grasp it. But as soon as you try to grasp it…

Thomas: It's gone. I suppose I don't mean that we necessarily resist it, but we don't go and do it again. For example, nature… when you go for a hike in the woods…

Monk: Thomas! You don't do it again. You can't do it again. Because it didn't come from you.

Thomas: Right… but a lot of those moments come from time in nature, in solitude, in quiet.

Monk: Sometimes they do, that's true. But you can't count on going into nature… It's like going into contemplation and counting on encountering God. Sometimes there's a period of dryness. A week, a day, a decade.

Thomas: But I guess what I was getting at is we don't even go and find nature again, even after we experience these moments. We stay away from the quietness.

Monk: That's what I was saying about the monasteries. That's the whole point. We're deathly afraid to listen. We're deathly afraid of the quiet that makes us listen. And the Spirit of God casts out fears because the Spirit of God knows the depths of God… and therefore knows the depths of you. I love those little surprises, ya know?

Thomas: Yeah.

Monk: Driving along, you're thinking about errands you have to run or a recent book you read, then, all of a sudden, whoosh! It's like, "Here I am!" In Hebrew, here I am is "Hineni!" I visited Israel many years ago. I was passing by the cemetery and I say the prayer for the dead whenever I pass a cemetery. As I'm coming to the cemetery, I'm driving along, ya know, at a normal speed and, I usually know where they are generally, but sometimes they surprise me. I'm coming around the corner and I haven't seen the cemetery and all of a sudden I hear "Hineni!" I knew that somebody in there needs my prayers. And God said, you don't have to know who they are. I do. … just let it happen. Here I am Lord. Here He is!

Thomas: Do you… do you ever pray for someone who you don't really know… you don't know much about them, but you can imagine that they have struggles and need prayers?

Monk: Oh, sure.

Thomas: They're a parent or they're alone.

Monk: Yes. And that's one of the gifts of monastic contemplation. God gives you people to pray for. Long before you meet them, God guides you to pray for them. One young man – I had been praying for him for decades before we met. He was addicted to everything you can be addicted to. Now, I always remind that young man, "Long before I met you, God gave you to me." I didn't know who he was until I met his mother. She was desperate for someone to help her son. This mother pressed her son's picture to my chest so hard that it gave me a black and blue mark. She stared at me and begged, "Save my son!" And when she said his name, it was like God just hit me over the head with a cast iron frying pan. I had heard her voice saying his name twenty years before I ever met her. Before her son was even born. I heard her saying his name 20 years before that meeting.

Thomas: Wow!

Monk: Not knowing who this kid was or what was going to be asked. And then I found out what it was and I'm saying, "God, what are you doing to me? Please! Give him to somebody else!" Oh no.

Thomas: Hahaha!

Monk: Oh no!

Thomas: Does He give you the why, too, or no?

Monk: No.

Thomas: He doesn't give you the whole picture, right?

Monk: No. You gotta listen to His son speaking. But my first encounter with that kid, I almost killed him…

Thomas: This I have to hear!

Monk: This kid had been to rehab after rehab. Addicted to just about every destructive behavior you can think of. And even some you probably couldn't think of! And he had just escaped from the latest rehab.

Thomas: Seriously?

Monk: Yes. I met his mother through a friend of a friend – at a dinner event. We had never met before. That's where she pressed this kid's picture into my chest. After that attack, I didn't hear from her for a while… I started thinking maybe I'm off the hook here. Then the kid comes home from the latest rehab. It's February. It was Lent. I'm fasting. If it hadn't have been Lent and I hadn't been fasting, Thomas, I would have killed him on the spot. And I can tell you that without any hesitation. She calls him over… and of course from this kid's perspective, here's another holy man my mother's dragging into my life. My father just betrayed me. Taking me on vacation but then locked me up in a camp. All I need is another old man messing around in my life. Add that to his natural attitude, okay, and you've got a mix for disaster. It's February. He's in cut-off pants and sandals. February. He's got a do-rag with a skull on it. With all his skull paintings plastering the walls of his room. He opens the door, just this much. I said, "I'm not sure why I'm here either, but your mom thinks…" He just turns around, away from me. I go in. I'm talking to him. I'm not preaching to him. Wouldn't work with me. Not going to work with him!

Thomas: Right.

Monk: Too intelligent for that. He was so cynical. He was so insulting. He was… I had to give him an answer for every possible motive for my being there. And this went on, Thomas, for two and a half hours. I got there at 9 o'clock. It was 11:30 at night. I hadn't eaten. Remember, it was Lent and I was fasting. It was so hot in that room and I had a cold. If I wasn't fasting, alright, second sentence out of his mouth, I would've had to walk out of the room because of the way he was talking to me. So finally, just sheer weariness. I'm sitting in front of the window. And he's pulled up a stool in front of me, as far away from me as he could get.

Thomas: This is two and a half hours into it?

Monk: Two and a half hours into it! And I was sweating.

Thomas: Was he looking at you most of the whole time?

Monk: With that confrontational and dismissive look. You know!

Thomas: Right.

Monk: Even despite the fasting, I was becoming angry. This had to stop or it was going to end up a tragedy. A tragedy of me not being able to help. Finally… I said to this kid, "I don't know what else I can tell you. I'm available because God seems to be insisting that I be available to you. Your mother seems to think, and mothers know these things, she seems to think I can be of some sort of help. I can't go on with this. I can't spar with you anymore. Your mom has my number. If you think I can be of help, you give me a call." I was angry at God… I started to get up and this kid puts his hand around my neck. He puts his head against mine and he said, "Bro, don't leave me or I'll die." I wish he had never said that, Thomas. I wish he had never said that… because there was no getting away after that. That was confirmation. *"Save my boy!"* And I wasn't going to get off the hook for this for the rest of my life with what God wanted to do for this kid. And the battles. You know! He was with me almost every day for a year. I fed him. I took him places. He went everywhere with me. The rehabs. And the whores he was sleeping with. Whose brothers were supplying him with drugs.

Every time there was one step forward, there were five steps backward. I would beg God, isn't there somebody else better for this kid? No, Brother, he's yours. I gave him to you before he was born. But he finally got… the one thing that saved this kid is that he believed in the mysticism. He believed in the power of the Sacraments. He went to confession every two weeks when he was with me. And I took him to mass with me all the time. Because that's where the saving is done. I'm the garden hose. The lawn doesn't need the hose, it needs the water. Matter of fact, leave the hose too long on the lawn, it'll ruin it. Do good and disappear. But that's what saved him. Why do I give up every aspect of my schedule to help this kid? Why? Why does he have unlimited access to me? Why? Because… Your fault! [pointing up towards God]

But that's the way it is with contemplation. All the suffering that I went through before meeting him… maybe I went there just for this. God's not beyond wasting 4 years of my life just to deal with some lost and confused brat. But, you see, that's the pattern. Some people say, *"How?"* You're asking me *how*? This is what I had to go through in this particular odyssey. And this is only one of several dozen people who God has given me along the way. I have no idea where they come from. What is the process? Ha Ha Ha! Listen!

Thomas: It goes counter to what we want, right? We want a step 1, 2, 3, 4. Oh, you missed step 2!

Monk: And that happened at a time that I was going through some terrible experiences…. But that's the time God had to choose. He had to choose a time when I was suffering to be able to touch what this kid was going through. And the frustration being put upon by forces that I couldn't control. So, what is the process? And what, are you going to tell this story every time? It's totally in the hands of the One… and it's not determinism, either, or predestination, or fatalism. You have to say yes, or God will not use you.

Thomas: Right.

Monk: Witness all the frustrated lives around us.

Thomas: Does He have a backup plan, then? Or not really? Ha! I don't know… He must… right?

Monk: Who? God? God always gets what He wants. If not you, then somebody else… I'm convinced this kid was going to be saved. If it wasn't me, it was going to be somebody. God's not going to let… God's not going to be able to face Mamo on the last day!

Thomas: Ha! That's great!

Monk: Or even His own mother!

14. Give All My Money Away?

Thomas: How generous does God really expect me to be? Am I supposed to give all my money away?

Monk: What do you mean?

Thomas: Can you be Christian and own a business?

Monk: Of course.

Thomas: Really? I've heard otherwise!

Monk: Jesus tells you to share some of your bread with the poor. That implies that you're getting your bread from some place, that you're not stealing it. To be able to give, you have to have. *Nemo dat quod non habet!* You can't give what you don't have.

Thomas: I've heard that before.

Monk: Yes, from me!

Thomas: That could be! So it's okay to have, but you should do good things with what you have?

Monk: The standard capitalist of the New Testament, Joseph of Arimathea; he was a pharisee and a very rich man… and he provided a tomb for Jesus. The Gospel points out that he believed in Jesus and he was a charitable man. Jesus goes after… you know the stories of Lazarus letting the guy starve… He goes after him. Why? Jesus goes after greed.

Thomas: Hmmm.

Monk: Like I've said before, you have two coats, your brother has none. That coat belongs to him by right. That's part of God's providence. That's why there's world hunger. We dump billions of bushels of wheat into the ocean to preserve what we think is control over economics. The hypocritical cry to heaven for vengeance when the world is starving!

Thomas: We throw away massive amounts of food. I notice it every single day. Every kid that comes to my house, it seems, they take more food than they'll really eat. They'll ask for a whole bagel, take a few bites, and then be done with it. They'll want to throw it away.

They do the same thing with pizza crust. Throw it away.

Monk: That's right.

Thomas: If you don't correct them, guide them, they will do that. They throw away massive amounts of food.

Monk: Who's objecting to it? Are their parents teaching them otherwise?

Thomas: No. I don't think so.

Monk: After disrespect, the greatest sin for an Italian boy, okay, is to disrespect Almighty God's providence by throwing away food. If there's something left over, you can make something with it.

Thomas: Right.

Monk: You know how far a hundred dollars' worth of groceries can go? People that visit me say, "You're amazing with food, you're so resourceful." I can get by longer on a hundred dollars of groceries than most people go on three hundred. *Che non sprecare, che non se manca!* You don't waste it, you won't lack it.

Thomas: I like that expression. Italian?

Monk: Right!

Thomas: I think a lot of parents are more concerned with their kid overeating than they are about the kid not wasting food.

Monk: Yeah. There's a solution to that. It's called Little League.

Thomas: Oh, you mean actually do something? Be active?

Monk: Round out your child for crying out loud, instead of giving him a cell phone and letting him sit on the couch for six hours a day.

Thomas: Yeah, but it seems like a lot of parents are more concerned with… "You're full. Don't overeat." And it sounds like you're saying, "Take what you're going to eat. Don't waste what you've been given."

Monk: Yes.

Thomas: Am I wrong in thinking that Jesus would say, "You do what is right. Don't try to get someone else to do what is right." I guess both, probably?

Monk: You SAW me hungry and you fed me. Don't go feed the

whole world, but do feed the people Christ sends into your life.
Thomas: So we're to help the ones who cross our path?
Monk: God sends them into your life! They don't just cross your path. There are no coincidences in the Kingdom of God.
Thomas: Oh, right. Did I ever tell you that I met a man in McAllen, Texas? It's right on the Rio Grande River, near the southern most tip of Texas.
Monk: Why do I know McAllen, Texas? Maybe I have someone there on my Christmas list.
Thomas: Could be. Well, I spoke at a conference in McAllen and met a man who made me incredibly uncomfortable.
Monk: Good. He's doing God's work!
Thomas: Making me uncomfortable?
Monk: Absolutely. Comfort the afflicted. Afflict the comfortable. The truth challenges. Rarely do we encounter truth and walk away comfortable. Comforted? Perhaps. But comfortable? Oh no!
Thomas: Wow!
Monk: Wow is right. Their response to Jesus 2,000 years ago was beyond *"Wow!"* The Jesus so many people are peddling today, the hippie Jesus, the meek and gentle Jesus, the Mr. Rogers Jesus, you don't kill that guy. The people who encountered Jesus, they had to respond to Him. The same is true today. As one Rabbi put it, "God is not nice. God is not an uncle. God is an earthquake." That Jesus… *that* Jesus elicits a response. A powerful response. Even today, you either follow him or you kill him. Kill his influence in your life. Kill the things that remind you of him. Kill the traditions that remind you of him, that afflict your comfortableness. That… that has not changed… My apologies, Thomas, please tell me about McAllen.
Thomas: No apology necessary. What you just described… the earthquake and eliciting a response… a man in McAllen gave me that exact experience.
Monk: How so?
Thomas: I was speaking at a conference and Bob was supposed to

introduce me. As we talked, I found out that he loves to travel, but doesn't any more. Naturally, I asked why. He explained that he has several young children living in his home. Usually four or five. Are they his grandchildren? No. Whose children? He said he doesn't know.

Monk: Intriguing. Who are these children?

Thomas: That's just it. Not his. He doesn't know the kids at all, but they live with him for a few weeks. He opens his home, feeds them, takes care of them, and then they move on.

Monk: What?

Thomas: Every few days he gets a call, usually in the middle of the night, 2am, 4am. The caller asks Bob if he can take in another child. A young child was found on the northern shore of the Rio Grande river near McAllen. For about 1,000 miles, the Rio Grande forms the natural border between Texas and Mexico. Bob explained that U.S. border patrol will find children deserted along the north shore of the river. Bob gets a call every few days to see if he can take in another child.

Monk: Hmmm. How old are these children?

Thomas: He showed me pictures. Most of the kids he takes in are a few years old, but the youngest have been under 1-year-old. They are found wandering on the bank of the river or perhaps lying in a plastic float. Something you'd use in a swimming pool. They have nothing with them. No possessions. Just the clothing on their backs. Often with a phone number and name written all over their clothing. The phone number might be a family member or friend who lives in the US. Or something unspeakable…

Monk: These children are all alone! And this man takes them in…

Thomas: Right. He takes them in for a few weeks. Treats them as if they were his own children. He told me that he and his wife haven't taken a vacation for several years. He's semi-retired, a time in life when a lot of people do some traveling, but they choose to stay home so they can care for these children. Just imagine a 3-year-old traveling for hundreds – or even thousands – of miles before being dropped off on the bank of a river in the middle of the night. Then strangers take the child to Bob's home. He takes care of them for a few weeks while their next destination is decided.

Monk: And what is that next destination?

Thomas: I asked about that. He said that it depends. Some of these children are taken to a family member or friend who already lives in the US. Some of these children are used as a way to sneak in to the country. Sometimes they find that the contact information on the child's clothing is linked to a sex trafficking operation…

Monk: Oh no!

Thomas: Yes. Heart-breaking.

Monk: Where do those children go?

Thomas: He told me that there are foster programs and childcare organizations that will find long-term homes for them. But these kids, most of them are coming from south and central America. Most of them are just traveling through Mexico to get to the US. They've traveled, I guess it's over a thousand miles. Bob told me he used to love traveling, seeing the world, but now… his eyes lit up when he told me this. He said he'll take "his" kids for walks to the local playgrounds. An indescribable joy exuded from Bob as he told me this. It was absolutely contagious! He said, "It's like taking a kid to Disney World! These kids, when they see one of our little local playgrounds for the first time, they're so excited, it's like reliving Christmas morning from when my own kids were little." I remember him shaking his head in disbelief and telling me, "I am blessed, Thomas, I am blessed!"

Monk: Indeed he is. And a blessing to those children in their time of need.

Thomas: Uncomfortable, Brother. On my flight home, I found myself in tears on the plane several times. I don't do that, Brother. I don't take kids in. I don't open my home and share my life with strangers.

Monk: Hmmm.

Thomas: I started to formulate some excuses over the next few days. Bob's example made me so uncomfortable that I began to justify… Made up my own series of stories about why he could do this, but I couldn't…

Monk: I see. And now you're beating yourself up?

Thomas: Yeah, a little. Okay, maybe a lot. My excuses, my justifications, that was my way of killing the example. Killing the uncomfortableness. Brother, I don't do what Bob does. [long silence] I don't…

Monk: I understand. Believe me, I understand what you are saying, what you are feeling.

Thomas: You do? So what do I do about it? What's my role?

Monk: You saw me homeless and you took me in. Welcome to my Kingdom. You saw me homeless and you didn't take me in, go to Hell. Do not pass go, do not collect $200. Period.

Thomas: Then people in that area who don't take kids in… well, I guess they might not realize that so many children are in need in their own backyard.

Monk: What about them?

Thomas: What are they called to do?

Monk: Do they have the same opportunity this man has to administer to the suffering Christ?

Thomas: I guess they do.

Monk: Do they do it?

Thomas: But so do I. I have that opportunity – yet I don't do what Bob does.

Monk: Are kids being dropped off in your town?

Thomas: No.

Monk: Well then God didn't send them into your life.

Thomas: But there are people in my town or in my area who need help like that.

Monk: Yeah, so? See what you can do to help them. Take 10% of your income and give it to Christ.

Thomas: And look for it?

Monk: Again, I emphasize the "you SAW me" part. Okay? Get involved with your heart instead of just your wallet.

Thomas: Yes.

Monk: Jesus doesn't want you to give from what you're not going to miss. If you have to give something of your heart, then you're invested in this "Christ-child" if you will.

Thomas: What about voting for people to do what you want done?

Monk: In the place of you doing it? I think you know that answer.

Thomas: From a capability perspective, as a country, the US is capable of helping so many more people than we do. But so are we as individuals!

Monk: God's not going to stand America in front of Him on the last day. He's going to say YOU saw me hungry, what did you do? This is the job of the Christian, not the government.

Thomas: I've always wondered, is that why Jesus didn't ignore political questions, but it wasn't the bulk of His conversation.

Monk: He wouldn't get snared in that. Don't forget, the Jews didn't want God coming in. They wanted the Romans out. That's what they wanted in a Messiah.

Thomas: He wouldn't get caught up in their game of …

Monk: "… and He went and hid because they wanted to make him King…" How many times do you read that in the Gospel.

Thomas: Right.

Monk: When Pilate says, "Oh, you're a king? Then how come you've you been hiding from these people who want to make you king? And Jesus says, "Because my kingdom is not of this world." The way you spell K-I-N-G and how I spell K-I-N-G are two entirely different things!

Thomas: Hmm.

Monk: My final prayer before going to bed last night was the Office of Vigils. There's the announcement of Emmanuel. "The virgin shall conceive and bear a son. And they'll call him wonder counselor, father forever." You look at that and you say, "They're going to call Emmanuel father forever? I thought the Father was sending him? And you read in the notes of The American Catholic Study Bible… Get the American Catholic Study Bible. It explains everything that is obscure. It is the best. The best.

Thomas: I think I might own a copy!

Monk: It says, what does this mean, they're calling him father forever? What it means is that He will, like a father, never abandon his people, this Emmanuel. He is going to be "God with us" permanently. He's not doing this as a demagogue or a leader. He's coming as a father. And a father does not abandon his children… Except, of course, in modern times where people decide that the grass is greener somewhere else.

Thomas: So His challenge is always an individual challenge. Always. It's always a personal, "You…"

Monk: It has to be. It has to be, Thomas. Do we have a collective responsibility as a Church? Yes. Yes. Should we send money to refugee kids who are persecuted across the globe? Absolutely.

Thomas: So that counts under the "See me hungry", even though you may not see them personally. You have been made aware of their plight. Via the news, via an article…

Monk: *They* have been made known to *you.*

Thomas: Is it realistic to pick one cause, rather than every single cause that is made know to you? Do for one what you wish you could do for everyone?

Monk: Like everything else in life, Thomas, all the gifts you've been given, you have to decide where to use them. It's the same reason a man chooses one woman out of the 10 he's dated. You fall in love. Nothing can sustain here, unless there's an abiding love.

Thomas: You fall in love with the cause? You can fall in love with just one cause?

Monk: You fall in love with the Christ who says, "Here I am."

Thomas: The Christ in them.

Monk: Yes, Thomas. You see Christ in them. Christ who comforts you and challenges you, often at the same time! If love doesn't cost you anything, is that really love? Aquinas defined agape love as willing the good of the other as other. Not choosing to do something for the other because of what it might get you in return! Will the good. Willing something entails choosing to want what's best and then acting on that. Not wishful thinking. Not hoping someone else might do something. You. Loving. You taking action. Even when it hurts. Love even when it hurts!

Thomas: Brother, I think I have some work to do.

Monk: Don't we all. And that's why I say it over and over. Let Him love you. Let His love flow into you. Let His love flow through you and out towards those He puts on your path.

Thomas: Last week I was talking to a confirmation class about the miracle of the feeding of the 5,000 in the Gospels. There's a little boy there with the bread and fish.

Monk: We read about it in Matthew yesterday.

Thomas: At the end, He told them to gather up everything so that nothing would be wasted.

Monk: Same thing here.

Thomas: Right. We were talking about those two things: there's a little boy who had some food and God asked for it… I don't know what the boy does at the end of that day, does he go home and say Jesus took my fish? He took probably everything the kid had for lunch, or maybe it was lunch for his parents or grandparents.

Monk: He was probably there selling fish.

Thomas: Could be.

Monk: He had 5 loaves. What's a kid going to do with 5 loaves?

Thomas: They were big?

Monk: Yeah, sure!

Thomas: Either way, God said give me what you have. Jesus said I need that and then I'll do something amazing with it. His miracle came through people. Like when you helped that kid with his addictions, it came through you. You were that garden hose. God could have said, I need a hose. I'm going to get a hose. Brother, you were the hose God chose! And then He did not waste anything!

Monk: Tommy, you're something else! I was sorry to see that it was Matthew's version yesterday because for the discussion that we're having there's a very important line that John has in his account that's not here in Matthew. It's Phillip who comes to Him and says that the people are two days in the desert and Jesus says to him, "Feed them yourselves."

Thomas: I thought that was great.

Monk: And that's how we know they bought the fish from the boy, 200 days wages couldn't feed them. Well, what do you have? We have this kid over here with fish… okay, give me what you do have. Freely, for the purpose of God. There's always a multiplication.

Thomas: So how much do I give? How generous does God want me to be?

Monk: The Pharisees asked, "Should we pay the coin to Caesar?"

Thomas: Give to Caesar what is Caesar's and to God what's God's!

Monk: Ah! And how do you interpret that? What is Jesus saying there? And, by the way, it's Jesus asking the question. Not only of the Pharisees, but of us, here, today!

Thomas: Hmmm. Well, what is God's?

Monk: Who's image is on the coin?

Thomas: Caesar's.

Monk: Right. And who's image is on you?

Thomas: God's. So I'm supposed to be more generous than I am!

Monk: Uh Huh. I'm asking what is Jesus asking you? What is He saying to you about this? About generosity?

Thomas: Step it up!

Monk: In what way?

Thomas: Many! That's a little discomforting. I could be much more generous in a lot of ways. With money. Time. Talents.

Monk: Hmmmm. No kidding! And we're afraid of newness nowhere more than when it comes to God. Because we don't want to change. If we want to change, we certainly don't want Him to change us. Because we don't trust His agenda.

Thomas: Trust! There it is again.

Monk: Do you know Saint Faustina? The Polish sister who…

Thomas: Sure. The painting. Divine Mercy!

Monk: Yes! She had visions of Christ and He asked her to commission that painting.

Thomas: I've seen it. Above her tomb in Krakow. Close to Oskar Schindler's factory.

Monk: And the words Christ wanted inscribed on the painting…

Thomas: "Jezu Ufam Tobie"… Polish for "Jesus, I trust in You."

Monk: There you go. Should you be more generous? With what? In what ways? Ask Him. And listen!

Thomas: And then trust. Jesus, I trust in you!

15. God is no Respecter of Democracy

Thomas: Isn't it time for the Church to make some changes? To keep up with the world?

Monk: Yes.

Thomas: Really?

Monk: And no.

Thomas: Of course. Here you go again! Two opposite answers is not an answer.

Monk: Thomas, you asked two entirely different questions. I simply answered both in the order you asked them.

Thomas: Yes, it's time to make changes and no, the Church shouldn't keep up with the world?

Monk: There you have it.

Thomas: Why not keep up with the world?

Monk: How do you change the world if you're the same as the world? Or, as Mother Angelica, the founder of EWTN, put it: "God wants you to be in the world, but so different from the world that you will change it. Get cracking!"

Thomas: You might have a point there… but, how do you influence the world if you don't relate to the world?

Monk: Hence the yes and no. Make changes – yes, but not in order to keep up with the world. Make changes in order to connect with, challenge, inspire and ultimately change the world.

Thomas: Governments change to keep up with the world. Democracies change.

Monk: And the Church is not a democracy.

Thomas: Why not? Why isn't the Church more of a democracy? You don't like the popular vote?

Monk: Where has it led?

Thomas: What do you mean?

Monk: Where has democracy led those who have worshipped it?
Thomas: Worshipped it?
Monk: Yes. You know very well that people often worship their politics.
Thomas: Sure, you have a point. A good point. A lot of people certainly act as if they worship their politics above all else.
Monk: Oh, we are very capable of worshipping just about anything. We worship sports, music, clothing, geography, moments in history, historical figures, careers, titles, stuff, even ideas – like democracy.
Thomas: And this is wrong?
Monk: Dead wrong. And deadly.
Thomas: Deadly?
Monk: Deadly to the soul. To what matters most. To life. To relationship with our Creator and with our very brothers and sisters.
Thomas: You're serious about this.
Monk: Incredibly serious. Whenever we worship something, love something in front of God, we get off course.
Thomas: And democracies get off course?
Monk: Of course they get off course. *"Off course"* is an excellent way to look at this. If you were planning to land on the moon, would you ask the public to vote on the best fuel? Or computer systems? Would you vote on the location of the guidance satellites or the aerodynamics of the rocket? Would you vote about the laws of physics?
Thomas: No. Definitely not! But…
Monk: But nothing. You're trying to get to God here. Ask Him the best way. That's not democracy. Not a popular vote. Sure, you can benefit from the experiences of others, but you wouldn't choose your advisors by a democracy, would you? A democracy tends to favor the loudest voices and the most popular voices. In your experience, are the loudest voices or the most popular voices usually the wisest voices, the most correct voices?

Thomas: Is loudness or popularity a good measure of what's best? I have to admit, no.

Monk: Thomas, immerse yourself in the lives of the saints. Why? They consistently answered a question posed repeatedly by Saint Benedict.

Thomas: Which question?

Monk: One of life's most important. A question we've already discussed, but one worthy of revisiting often. Do you seek God?

Thomas: From a democratic perspective, do most people seek God?

Monk: That's not God's question for you. His question is personal. Do you? You see, Thomas, our God is a big fan of personal responsibility. Imagine a family with three young children. Would the parents be wise to run that family as a democracy? What would the family's bank account look like if all purchasing decisions were made by a 3-2 vote with the majority of the voters under the age of 5? What groceries would make it into the shopping cart?

Thomas: Oh boy! But that's why there's an age limit for voters in a democracy.

Monk: Age, yes, but isn't it a lot more than that?

Thomas: You're not a fan of democracy?

Monk: Thomas, Thomas, Thomas! Again, it's a tool. Just like any other tool, democracy has its functions, its usefulness, its purpose. However, it is not the recommended tool in the quest for God.

Thomas: You're something else. I know I've said that many times before, but it's worth repeating. You. Are. Something. Else! Is it possible to find a topic where you don't have a strong opinion?

Monk: My dear Thomas! God is the author of Truth with a capital T. Fallacies may become fashionable, but they are still fallacies. At the core, we all know this. Consensus does not make the untrue true. If 1,000 people stand up and say something stupid, it's still stupid.

Thomas: Can you give me a practical example?

Monk: Easily. But I'm not letting you off that easily. I'll give you one example and then you give me one.
Thomas: Deal.
Monk: Parenting. The popular approaches, fashionable approaches change often. Just a small sampling of the fashions: Children should be seen and not heard. Send kids off to boarding school around the age of 10. Spank your children. Never spank your children. Guide your children. Let your children find their own path. You'll do it my way because I'm the mother. We'll do whatever you feel like doing, sweetie. Eat together as a family. Rarely eat together as a family. No TV. Limited TV. Unlimited TV. No cell phones. Unlimited cell phone use but not until age 12. Call adults Mister or Misses. Call adults by their first names. Spend a lot of money to demonstrate your love. Spend a lot of time together to demonstrate your love. All of these have been fashionable at some time in some place.
Thomas: Aren't these just different approaches?
Monk: They are, but many of them are also fallacies that have become fashions. Democracy… That was your initial question. Would you take a vote on the best bed time for your children? Or the amount of schooling your children receive? Or the amount of ice cream your children eat each week? Would you allow the children a full vote? Half a vote? Would only those who live in your neighborhood be allowed to vote? Or in your country? Or your continent? Would you poll people who lived in past centuries? What's popular is ever-changing. What's right is never-changing.
Thomas: You don't value democracy as much as I do.
Monk: *Au contraire mon frère!* I'm just trying to be honest about its limitations as a tool. Democracy, as Churchill put it, is the worst form of government except for all those other forms that have been tried from time to time! Your turn, Thomas.
Thomas: I'll play along. Smoking. That's an easy one. It was incredibly fashionable for years. It still is in some countries.

Monk: There you go.

Thomas: Here's another… burning witches at the stake. That was popular. Dueling by sword or pistol was once a popular means for settling disputes.

Monk: Look at you!

Thomas: How about… uh-oh, I'm not sure you'll like this one… Christians converting non-Christians by force. That's certainly been popular, a fashionable fallacy!

Monk: Now you're enjoying this. Good.

Thomas: You like that one? I thought you'd defend or argue.

Monk: No. Fallacies can even become fashionable in the Church. Nietzsche made that point even more strongly when he said that there was only one Christian and he died on the cross.

Thomas: Wow! I've never heard that.

Monk: You see, we're back to the sheepdog principle. Point people towards the Shepherd. The Way. The Truth. The Life.

Thomas: Which might be different from the popular way. The popular truth. The popular life.

Monk: Might be? *MIGHT* be? Thomas, it's consistently and radically different. We are rebels who must lay down our arms.

Thomas: Rebels? I love it when you get all worked up about this stuff! The passion, Brother. Don't lose that!

Monk: Passion? Worked up? Thomas, this is a battle for souls. Catherine of Siena, one of the toughest women in all of history and one of the wisest, she challenged people of her time and all time. Saint Catherine said, "Be who God meant you to be and you will set the world on fire." Pursuit of truth is an eternal question… with eternal consequences. Passion, indeed! Catherine also said "Dio considera le anime più delle città!" "God cares more about souls than cities!" That woman said so much. Thomas, drink deeply from the lives of the saints, especially that bold woman!

Thomas: Is this part of the reasoning behind all the Christian denominations?

Monk: Sure. Where two or three are gathered in My name, we incorporate.

Thomas: Ha!

Monk: And splinter after splinter after splinter. The tragedy is that's the one thing the Catholic Church was always protected against.

Monk: Thomas, do you remember the story of David and Goliath?

Thomas: Sure. I think everyone knows that story.

Monk: What's the story? Can you give me the short version?

Thomas: Yeah. Goliath was a giant, an extremely large warrior. David was a kid, a shepherd boy. Goliath challenged the soldiers on David's side. The Israelites, right? Sounds all too familiar.

Monk: Yes.

Thomas: Goliath challenged the Israelites to a mono e mono battle. One on one. They saw his size and no one volunteered. Until finally this little kid, this shepherd boy named David, stepped up. He hit the giant with a rock and killed him. Then David became king. That's the story, as far as I remember. I'm sure there's more to it.

Monk: What are we to learn from this story?

Thomas: You're asking me? I suppose that the underdog can win. And bring rocks to all your fights.

Monk: Very funny.

Thomas: Step up.

Monk: Tell me more about that.

Thomas: David knew who the enemy was and confronted that enemy.

Monk: Hmmm.

Thomas: You like to say Hmmm.

Monk: Maybe I do. Hmmm.

Thomas: I think I know what your Hmmm is about. David knew and confronted the enemy. You're asking me if I know and confront my enemy. If I face reality and then address what needs to be addressed.

Monk: [smiling, nodding] And?

Thomas: My turn to say Hmmm. Sometimes. Not often enough. Sometimes I know the enemy but don't confront. Sometimes I confront what's not the enemy.

Monk: Both humbly seeking and acting on the truth. Rare. Thomas, do I need someone to tell me I'm wrong when I know I'm wrong? Or do I need someone to tell me I'm wrong when I think I'm right? Do I need guidance when I'm on the right path? Or do I need guidance when I'm lost? We need Christ and His church and His followers to let us know we're on the wrong path especially when we think we're on the right one. Ask your Heavenly Father what He wants you to confront. And then listen!

16. The Bible: True or False?

Thomas: Is the Bible true?
Monk: What do you mean by true?
Thomas: Well, is it real. Is it accurate? Is it true? Do you think that everything in the Bible actually happened?
Monk: Ahhh! Thomas, do you remember our conversation about bad things happening to good people?
Thomas: Of course! I think I now get why people can do bad things, and why natural disasters exist… but I'm still not clear on why we have to have things like cancer.
Monk: Because we have the opportunity not to, and we chose to kill each other instead.
Thomas: But why does it have to even exist at all? Or does it?
Monk: It does not have to exist at all. Given that the human condition has been torn away from the source of life, the tree of life, where there was no disease. Well, man chose… he wanted another way. Well, you got your other way. So all the defenses that the tree of life represents, are no longer available to because you don't rely on the power of that tree, and it's wisdom.
Thomas: That story is a lot like the story of creation,
Monk: It is the story of creation. That's the only inkling we have about the mystery…
Thomas: But that story… was it really two people in a garden? Really?
Monk: The human race began with one male and one female. Okay? Adam and Eve? Garden?
Thomas: Doesn't matter what they were called?
Monk: Billions of years ago?
Thomas: Yeah?
Monk: Because the Bible is absolutely the truth. It is not factual.
Thomas: What? How do you tell somebody that?
Monk: Because they think the only thing that is factual is empirical.

Thomas: So it happened, but not necessarily…
Monk: God created man and woman. How did He do it? How should I know? He's… He's the infinite God. Took six days? Took billions of years?
Thomas: But!!!! Doesn't that open it up, can't a person then question anything in the Bible?
Monk: They can't question the truth. They can question the details or the facts. You can't question that God made man.
Thomas: Right. But can you question…
Monk: That's your answer.
Thomas: But can you question whether Jesus said the things He's quoted as saying?
Monk: Can you question whether Jesus said something or not? It's been recorded by people who heard Him. Can you question it? Sure you can.
Thomas: Okay. So they were not stretching or changing things?
Monk: No. Jesus said it. They recorded it. They didn't interpret it.
Thomas: But they didn't write it down for years.
Monk: Sometimes. And sometimes there are things attributed to Jesus that you can't find anywhere else in the Bible. Saint Paul says that Jesus says it's more blessed to give than receive. Jesus never says that in the Gospels.
Thomas: But they couldn't have written down everything He said.
Monk: That's what Saint John says. He said, "These and many other things Jesus did and said, if they had been recorded, the whole world itself could not hold all the books." That's the basis of sacred tradition.
Thomas: How did Paul know so much? I mean, Jesus appeared to him, but did He fill him in on everything?
Monk: He filled him in on a lot of things. Paul's knocked off his horse, he's got to be wondering where he went wrong. Then he consulted with the apostles…

Thomas: So a lot of what he wrote probably came from them? Came from Peter and…

Monk: A whole community of followers. Ananias was the guy who first dealt with Paul after he was knocked off his horse. But don't forget, Paul was going to a Christian *community* in Damascus… to make arrests.

Thomas: Right.

Monk: It wasn't like he just talked with one guy who believed in Christ.

Thomas: So *they* taught him? *They* filled him in? The earliest Christians.

Monk: Essentially, he understood it. As it says in the Acts of the Apostles, "The scales fell from his eyes." What does that mean? It means that finally he said, "This all makes sense."

Thomas: So you have to translate the Bible based on how it was written? The Noah Flood thing… that could be a little bit off?

Monk: I don't believe the flood actually happened.

Thomas: No?

Monk: Not in the terms of the Bible. Was there a flood? Yeah. Everybody says there was. All the cultures do. Was it God punishing the world? No. Because I don't believe God punishes.

Thomas: So why would the Bible say that?

Monk: I have no idea. What does it say? I'm sorry that I made the human race? Oh, God can reverse a decision?

Thomas: So you think the Bible writers got it wrong?

Monk: What? It's not a matter of getting it wrong, Thomas. You're missing the point. The point is that there's a truth there. Get the facts wrong, get the details wrong, but don't miss the truth.

Thomas: I got it.

Monk: I have to laugh every time these people say, "Oh, we found the Arc!" This I gotta see!

Thomas: A lot of people use that to get away from the Bible, to say, "If anything's wrong with the thing, then maybe the whole thing is wrong."
Monk: They don't understand what the thing is. You want a textbook, go find a textbook. You want the Bible… the living Word of God… that's something entirely different.
Thomas: Do you want some more coffee?
Monk: Yes, please.
Thomas: Cream?
Monk: Yes. I always put the sugar in first, so it dissolves in the hot coffee before adding the cream.
Thomas: Of course you do! I like to warm the milk before adding coffee.
Monk: That's the Italian's job! He's the guardian of Truth and Beauty for the universe.
Thomas: Guardian of Truth and Beauty! That's rich.
Monk: We were on a very important track there before we got off on this tangent… which you engender with remarkable rapidity.
Thomas: I didn't get us off track.
Monk: Yes, you did! You went off on a "Well, what about this…" Wait! We have not finished that point yet!
Thomas: Fine. Guilty.
Monk: Moses, in his creation story, because all the people around him, the pagan people, say that their god created the world in a moon, a month, how does Moses say that ours is the real God? And He's much better!
Thomas: He did it quicker!
Monk: He did it in 6 days, not even a week, and rested on the 7th.
Thomas: And He was done.
Monk: That's how powerful He is!
Thomas: Ha ha! Is that why Moses made it 6 days?

Monk: Sure. Every scripture scholar knows this. And if we taught this, people would understand and stop trying to play creation games.

Thomas: What was the other religion that taught 30 days?

Monk: All the religions around them. The Sumarians, the…

Thomas: They all taught 30 days?

Monk: Well, the moon. The phases of the moon.

Thomas: Right. And there we have it, 7 days! Doesn't that suggest that the Bible might be inaccurate?

Monk: Henri de Lubac… very, very popular theologian in 1960s… he said "The Old Testament is a record of failed communication."

Thomas: I like that! The Old Testament is a…

Monk: A record of failed communication! God talks to Adam in the garden. Adam listens to the snake. God tells Abraham, "I'm going to make you the father of many nations." Abraham is 90 years old and he says, "Where's my baby?" God was saying something much different. Yes, there was a physical child involved, Isaac, but that's not what God was saying about making him a father of many nations. God talks to Moses. Moses gets lost for 40 years in the wilderness. God gives the covenant at Mount Sinai… while Moses is up there getting the Ten Commandments, the people are down in the valley making a golden calf and dancing around it. God tells David, "You are my chosen one…You're going to be my image in Israel." David goes and sleeps with Uriah's wife has Uriah killed in battle. Then the prophets. They all come up with a Plan B sort of thing. If God wanted to send us another book, another set of writings, He would've done that. He saw that it was going nowhere. And so what did He say? Jesus tells the story about the vineyard. The guy sends his servants with the orders. Finally he says, "Surely they'll respect my son." He had to come himself to set it straight. And that's when Jesus said, "I've not come here to abolish the law." *I'm here to tell you what it is. Because you've missed the whole point!*

Thomas: Oh, how history repeats itself. Didn't Mark Twain say that history never repeats itself, but it does often rhyme?
Monk: Indeed. You could look at the Bible like a mirror. Showing us who we are. Thomas, have you seen Caravaggio's painting? In the early 17th century, Caravaggio captured the essence of what we're talking about here. Of what it is to seek truth. His great work – well, he had so many of them – but one, the Incredulity of Saint Thomas, your namesake, captures our dilemma.
Thomas: How so?
Monk: The painting depicts the famous scene where Thomas puts his hand into the wound of the resurrected Christ. But there's a twist. If we look closely, it seems that Thomas doesn't want to put his hand into Christ's side. Another hand is pulling Thomas' hand. Not only that, but Thomas' face and body language betray him. This is doubting Thomas. He said that unless he put his fingers into the nail marks and his hand into Christ's side, he wouldn't believe. Well, here's his chance and he doesn't seem to want to do it. That Thomas said, essentially, give me evidence. Give me a reason to believe. This Thomas, two thousand years ago, even specified the evidence he was seeking. Well, Christ is giving him exactly what he demanded, and the painting depicts Thomas trying to avoid the evidence. Looking away. Not voluntarily putting his hand into the wounds.
Thomas: Ouch. It's what you said earlier about Pascal. Enough light to find what we want to and enough shadow to not find what we don't want to. In Caravaggio's painting Thomas was resisting, trying not to see.
Monk: Hmmm.
Thomas: A glimpse of human nature, indeed! A mirror to see who we are… So Christ's followers had doubts. They weren't perfect!
Monk: And Christ gave them exactly what they needed to make a choice. That's what Thomas' face – his whole being – says in Caravaggio's painting! Christ gave Thomas what he needed. And

He gives you and I everything we need, as well. How will we respond?

Thomas: That's a difficult thought.

Monk: That's reality. Father Benedict, my parish pastor from many years ago, used to say to me, "Brother, you will fall victim to one of two powers in the universe. And there's no escaping it."

Thomas: I can see a bit of myself in this painting.

Monk: Of course you can. And you should. Thomas, until you can see yourself in every character in every story, you have not truly encountered the story. Approach the Bible this way.

Thomas: Every character?

Monk: Yes. What is Thomas doing in this story?

Thomas: He doubts. He resists. But… he stays and lets Christ put his fingers into the wounds. He…

Monk: There you go. Ignatius of Loyola suggested using all 5 senses to imagine being in the Gospel stories as we contemplate them. Very powerful.

Thomas: I'm thinking about the other apostles. They watched this interaction between Thomas and Christ.

Monk: And Christ?

Thomas: I should see myself in His role, too?

Monk: Follow me. He says it over and over. Will you?

Thomas: Well, Christ is helping Thomas confront the Truth.

Monk: Ahhh.

Thomas: So you're saying that's my job, too…

Monk: Follow me.

Thomas: Not easy.

Monk: Should the Church teach what is easy, what is popular? Did Christ do and teach what was easy and popular?

Thomas: Brother, I can see myself resisting like Caravaggio's Thomas in the painting?

Monk: Christ takes your hand. As He takes mine. And speaks in our hearts. Follow me!

17. The "Wildness" of God & You

Thomas: It seems so complicated.
Monk: What? What seems so complicated?
Thomas: All of this stuff. Religion. Faith. History. Human nature. God. How does a normal person – a regular person just going about living life and trying to figure out all kinds of things, like work and parenting and money and making the mortgage payment… how does that person figure out God?
Monk: Oh. I see!
Thomas: Glad you do. Because I don't! I mean, we're busy. Too busy to spend all the time in the world digging in to this stuff. The stuff that you know. Stuff you could spend years…
Monk: Decades!
Thomas: There. That's my point. Too complicated.
Monk: But it's not, Thomas!
Thomas: No? Convince me of that!
Monk: Seek God. Not complexity.
Thomas: Okay. And? That's your answer?
Monk: When a theologian is explaining the faith, there is just what I've been talking about for years… Not making a guru from any theologian. Theologians are there to say, "This is what we know to be the truth, the end game. This is the mystic relationship that is… that is the Catholic faith, that is Christianity. Without sacraments, you have just another teacher. This is what it is. In the process of doing that, you look at the great theologians… some people were very, very precise. Like Thomas Aquinas, for instance, there's no fighting his logic. The man is brilliant. But that theology, okay, is not going to save anyone. But when you read the hymns that he wrote… he wrote the office for Corpus Christi, for the feast of the body and blood of Christ…
Thomas: Oh, I didn't know that.
Monk: And the exquisite… this man has seen the face of God.

Thomas: Did he write that, those hymns, towards the end of his life?
Monk: That's a good question. I think it's somewhere... Corpus Christi was 1264… Aquinas died a decade later. I would say, yes… somewhere, towards the end of his life. I think he did it while he was a professor in Paris, as a matter of fact.
Thomas: You could tell that he had experienced God?
Monk: Because he took you from the logic, this is the dogma, this is what we know to be the truth because God revealed it… This is what it means – which is also theology – and this is what it is for you and where it's leading you … to the completion that he has no way of touching. Words on paper might not call you to be outrageous. Logic might not call you to be outrageous. God does.
Thomas: God calls us to be outrageous?
Monk: Every one of us. You, Thomas, are called to be outrageous.
Thomas: I am?
Monk: You are. Meeting Father William McNamara – who, if you haven't read his books, then you are missing 99% of what I'm talking about.
Thomas: I think I have his book. Didn't he write *The Art of Being Human*? You referenced it in one of our conversations.
Monk: That's only one of his many books.
Thomas: That's the only one I've read.
Monk: Well, I guess having met him… have I ever told you about my encounter with him?
Thomas: You met him?
Monk: Oh yeah.
Thomas: Did you straighten him out?
Monk: No! Nova Scotia. I had read his books for years. And he calls the Holy Spirit the "Wildness of God" And unless you're willing to become a wild man, you'll never know the Spirit of God … who knows the depths of God which means He knows the depths of you. It was in Nova Scotia, in the darkness of winter. Bad, bad

winter. I was a Franciscan at the time and I was in my sandals. It was way up in North Kemptville, 7 miles in the woods. I trekked through the woods to get to the hermitage. I make it to this clearing. There's a lake and all these little hermitages. I see smoke coming out of the chimney at the big house. I looked like Doctor Zhivago, I was crusted with ice in my face and beard, my feet were bleeding. Freezing. I knocked on the door and Mother Tessa opens the door. I said, "Is Father William here?" She said, "Oh no, Brother. He lives up there." She points further up the mountain to a small hermitage. It's on the top of the mountain. There's smoke coming from that chimney, too. As I climbed towards his humble shack, he opens the door… I was at least 100 yards from him. He's standing there in his Carmelite Habit, big swirling thing. Thomas, I could see the burning in this man's eyes from where I was.

Thomas: Wow!

Monk: I'm looking at him, mesmerized by the snow swirling and the habit swirling and those wild eyes.

Thomas: That's God? That's the nature of God? The "Wildness of God"?

Monk: Wild! Not predictable. You don't put God in a little box or in a little book. And knowing about Him is simply not the same as knowing Him. This wild God made you to be the bearer of His image. Before He spun the planets off His fingers, He called out your name and said, "You are mine!"

Thomas: Why haven't I heard this?

Monk: Hmmm… That's a problem.

Thomas: Are you worried about the Church today? I mean, it seems like a lot is not going the right direction.

Monk: Anybody who's surprised by any problems, challenges, scandals in the Church doesn't know their history. Who of us doesn't fall short? Even Saint Paul said I do not do the good I want, but I do the evil I do not want. Problem is we don't put things in perspective. JP2 didn't die for my sins. Francis didn't die for my sins. Cardinal So and So didn't die for my sins. If the Church can survive the influence of fallen humanity we've had over centuries, the Church can survive! We have not taught people the faith. That they're here to seek God. Not to understand, but to be loved. There's no way we can understand the mystery. Nothing scratches the surface of the mystery. What can you say about God except God? Thomas, the job of the priests and theologians is to say this is what we know… as a springboard. It's an invitation into the mystery. If this is what we know and this is who you are, created by God. We've tried to make Christ palatable. He'll never be palatable. Ever. It takes an act of the Holy Spirit to be open to the mystery. We've taught people just stay out of jail and you're good. No! Every decision you make has to be made based on this identity. This is who you are, precious in the eyes of God. Once you see that, recognize the immensity of the saving power, then you start to see your brothers and sisters in the right light. We've turned love into this sentimental journey. When I'm feeling good, the sun is out, billowing through my windows, all is well with the world. But when I see the hideous cold, the real world that is what we deal with… I ache for something more. Thomas, they taught us as kids, not saying morning and night prayers was a great sin. Family that prays together stays together. We've gotten away from this. We teach, "she's a good person"… Sure, she's living w/ her boyfriend, but… Nonsense! We start distancing ourselves from the mystery. We become non-believing, non-practicing Catholics. If we were, there would be no such thing as abortion. If they have no right to get out of the womb intact, what does it matter where they live or go to school? If God wanted to send us another book or set of ethics, He would've. We needed the intimacy. Christ is going to forgive me in the confessional and only there! Christ is going to feed me with His flesh and blood and only there! And it doesn't matter who the priest is. The theology is this… the God who made you for Himself is not going to let anything get in the way. People who have experienced the Church… Irish say you can't talk bad about Father… Italians don't have that problem. They've long understood that priests are far from perfect.

Thomas: There's your sheepdog analogy! What do I do with this mystery?

Monk: Thomas, there's a difference between mankind looking for truth and Truth – with a capital "T" – finding mankind!

Thomas: You can say that again.

Monk: Thomas, don't complicate it. Do you think God wants to play a bigger role in your life?

Thomas: That's frightening question, but I think we all know the answer.

Monk: Will you let Him?

Thomas: Sure, but…

Monk: But what?

Thomas: I have a lot of work to do…

Monk: Who doesn't?

Thomas: Right, but…

Monk: Enough with the but!

Thomas: Brother, I'm so far from perfect.

Monk: Thomas, I've met a lot of so-called Christians in my life. Still waiting to meet the perfect Christian. Where are they? Does God need perfect instruments? Where does this idea come from? Okay, maybe not perfect, but give me a break!

Thomas: But what about all the atrocities committed by so-called Christians, so-called followers of Christ, throughout history?

Monk: When the Babylonians took the Jews for 70 years… it was a pagan, Cyrus the Persian, who brought Israel back to the land and rebuilt the temple. Cyrus didn't believe in the God of Israel. God used him. It says it right there in the book of Isaiah, "*You* are my chosen instrument." *You!*

Thomas: Wow.

18. Parenting is Tough!

Thomas: Parenting stuff is some of the hardest.
Monk: Hmmmm… How so?
Thomas: What to say, when to say it. Everything!
Monk: Protect and prepare. Both! Thomas, you ever ask St. Joseph to pray for you? Or the Blessed Mother?
Thomas: I've been trying to figure that out. I mean, how to…
Monk: Right! Stop trying to figure it out. Do it! Ask them to pray for you as a father, as a parent.
Thomas: Yeah. Simple.
Monk: Do you *try* to get dressed before you leave the house or do you get dressed? Do you *try* to brush your teeth or do you brush your teeth? Do you *try* to eat meals daily or do you do it? Tommy, stop *trying* to pray and do it!
Thomas: Right, Brother.
Monk: So, you were saying?
Thomas: Parenting is tough.
Monk: Nobody promised easy. You want it to be easy?
Thomas: That's not what I'm saying. It's just… you always say, "Don't answer questions people aren't asking!" I like that. I love that – at least the concept. But, how do I do that with my own kids? They're not always asking questions about some of the most important things.
Monk: Ahhh! You're right. They don't come up with the question. They come up with a "What is this, Daddy?" type of question. First, determine, what *is* the question that *they're* asking? Remember St. Augustine here. Every single person you and I encounter has this thirst for lasting happiness. A restless heart. Sure, they might not use those words. But they're looking for a deep and abiding joy. A peace beyond all understanding. A yearning that nothing on this earth can satisfy. And, as a sheepdog, your job and mine is just to point towards the true. The good. The beautiful. The Shepherd.

Thomas: So help them translate their questions.
Monk: Right. Jesus' first words in John's Gospel: "What do you seek?" He's asking, "What are you looking for?" As if He doesn't know?
Thomas: Jesus knows all about our restless hearts!
Monk: Right. Better than we do.
Thomas: What do you mean by sheepdog?
Monk: Your job. And mine. Have you ever seen a sheepdog?
Thomas: Sure.
Monk: What's the job of the sheepdog?
Thomas: Keep the sheep away from danger?
Monk: The sheepdog is not the Shepherd! A sheepdog might be dirty, loud, on the outskirts, imperfect! But the sheepdog's job is to keep the sheep following the shepherd. Keep them from getting too far off track.
Thomas: Ahh! And that's why you say that's your job. And mine.
Monk: You don't get to be a shepherd. You don't get to be somebody's guru. The culture today loves holding up experts. Gurus. But a true sheepdog merely points towards what is good and true and beautiful. Even some priests want to be the famous one. The center of it all. That's not their role! Sheepdogs!!! Far from perfect but striving to point towards perfect.
Thomas: So what does a parent tell their kids?
Monk: Figure out what they're really asking. And help translate it into their words. They're looking for what's really true. They don't want some fake sense of happiness, do they? They see right through that! They want to win a game or get a good grade. Why? Made in God's image! Made for greatness. And He put these people in your life for a reason. Acknowledge before God that you are the most miserable of sinners and yet He has made you pivotal for the salvation of at least these people He has sent into your life... In Jesus' time, there were tens of thousands of blind people. Why did Jesus only cure 3. Leprosy was a scourge of the Middle East. Why

does Jesus only cure 13 lepers? Because those were the people who were sent into His life for Him to deal with. Thomas, you are not called to convert the world. But you are called to witness Christ to the individual people God sends into your life! And your family, especially your children…

Thomas: Oh wow.

Monk: Love them unconditionally. And point towards. Be a Sheepdog, Thomas. A sheepdog, not a shepherd! Tell your children, God loves you more than I can. I love you no matter what. Even when I don't like the way you're behaving. Or when I say no. But God – the Good Shepherd – loves you perfectly. I'm an imperfect father. But God's the perfect Father! Tell them, Thomas!

Thomas: Tell them. No matter what.

Monk: Jesus says, just be prepared. If your kid asks you for bread, you can't give them a stone. So do your homework. Pray for help. Pray for guidance. Pray for wisdom. Thomas, God didn't mess up when He made you! And your kids need to know that, too. You are exactly what God had in mind when He made you!

Thomas: Don't we all need that reminder! Pointing towards truth.. culturally, that's a battle. We tell kids to discover themselves. I guess if it's their true self, that's what we want.

Monk: Where are they going to go for their true self? Discover the true self with their phones, online, with their peers, with their teachers who are sometimes more lost than they are… So many people will give you ideas that are so far off track… they'll manipulate you through your entire life.

Thomas: If you don't help them figure out some of life's most important questions, then… well…

Monk: Then you're not doing your job! Tom, as a parent, if you don't guide your children… Feed them. People go where they are fed. 2,000 years ago and today. They need spiritual food. They need truth. They need what is real. Not some lie. Not something that might feel good for a moment and then leave them aching for sustenance. The risen Christ says to Peter, "Do you love me? Feed my sheep!" He wasn't saying to throw a pancake on the griddle for breakfast. He was saying "feed them!" Care for them. Give them what they truly need. People go where they're fed, Thomas! If we're not giving them the depth, the sustenance they truly seek, they'll go somewhere else. They'll hit the drive-thru. Fast food. Not what the soul aches for. But if we don't feed them what's true and good and beautiful… Thomas, why do I say "Let Him love you" so much?

Thomas: I guess because we need to hear it? I need to hear it…

Monk: Yes! And we find it so hard to believe. Thomas, let Him love you. And let His love flow through you and into your children. Let Him love them through you!

Thomas: Yes. When and how to be patient, understanding, firm…

Monk: Well, my response, my best advice when we need to lay down the law… is, "It's not my idea. God didn't ask me when he made the grass green." It's not my voice. It's God's. My job is not to be God in their life. It's to point them to God. Get them spending time with God. On their knees. Asking Him for guidance. Not me. Pointing them to what He said, what He taught, what He's still teaching today. To what He's doing today.

Thomas: Simple. When you talk about it, it seems so simple. But…

Monk: As a parent, you can get lost in the weeds. Of course! Get on your knees more often, Tommy. Go before Almighty God. And again, I've said this before… but get on your knees not as Tommy or Thomas. Not as a dad. Not as anything but a child of God. Let Him love you! He will not lead you astray. Let. Him. Love. You.

Thomas: (Silent. Reflecting.)

Monk: Let the Father love you. Then, as a father, you pray that His love flows through you and into your children. And He answers you, Thomas. *He answers you!*

Thomas: I… Yes… Umm, Brother, then there's all this practical stuff. It seems so small and insignificant in light of what you're describing, but it's… well, that's where I mess up. Over and over.

Monk: I see. Well, let's get the big stuff right, eh?
Thomas: Yeah.
Monk: Saint Paul, when he was in prison in Rome, awaiting a death sentence from that wicked Emperor Nero – Paul writes, "Have no anxiety at all…" What? No anxiety? You realize what I'm dealing with here? I've got a teenage daughter. No anxiety? I've got financial struggles. Just lost my job. Health crisis. No health insurance. No anxiety? Paul was awaiting his execution under one of Rome's most brutal emperors. Nero used Christians covered with tar as torches to light his parties. *No anxiety???*
Thomas: That's a high bar!
Monk: Then Paul says to pray… "and a peace of God that surpasses ALL understanding will guard your heart and mind…" A peace that surpasses understanding! That's the peace I want, Thomas. Is that the peace you're looking for here?
Thomas: Uh, yeaahhhh!
Monk: That – those words – Paul's words come from a man who spent a lot of time in prayer. People write books like "Don't sweat the small stuff." But they don't tell you the real secret. Because it's no secret. Get before your God. Kneel in the presence of the Almighty and let Him love you!
Thomas: Right. So get the big stuff right. It sounds petty, but then what do I do about the practical stuff?
Monk: There's nothing petty about the practical stuff. People asked Jesus questions all the time. Some were looking for answers, for guidance, but others – some had ulterior motives.
Thomas: My youngest daughter was really confused because her classmate was becoming a girl.
Monk: Becoming a girl?
Thomas: Right.
Monk: Becoming?
Thomas: That's what the school was telling everyone.
Monk: And? What did you say?

Thomas: She was really confused. And I actually took your advice. I prayed about it. A lot!

Monk: Hmmm.

Thomas: I asked my daughter if she was an elephant. My daughter thought that was funny. I said, "Could you pretend to be an elephant?" She said, "Sure! I love doing that!" I asked, "But, even if you were really good at pretending, would you actually be an elephant?" She called me silly! I said, "What if you made elephant ears and put them on your head? What if you had the coolest trunk and stuck it on your nose?" She said, "No way, daddy!" I asked, "What if you really really wanted to be an elephant, thought you were an elephant, even glued or sewed the ears and trunk onto your body? Then would you be an elephant?"

Monk: What did she say?

Thomas: She said, "No. No. No. But you can pretend. And that's fun!"

Monk: Sheepdog. There you go. It's not easy resisting a culture at war with the truth.

Thomas: You're telling me! I had this conversation with my daughter only because a good friend's daughter came home from college after her first semester and I had one of these wake-up calls. Suddenly, this young lady seems completely absorbed by this philosophy… There is no such thing as right or wrong. Everything is "outdated" or "old-fashioned." Her parents are… I guess intolerant was the word she used repeatedly. How can a parent pre-empt this?

Monk: Well, you can't fool mother nature. And you can't pre-empt everything. That doesn't mean there's nothing you can do.

Thomas: So my friends' daughter – the college freshman – is arguing with her parents that the Church is so outdated, that it's prejudiced, judgmental. Especially in the views of marriage, but she's attacking everything. Tradition is wrong. Rules are wrong.

She's all excited and now she's educated, so her parents need to get with the times!

Monk: Hmmm. Professing to be wise they became fools!

Thomas: What?

Monk: Saint Paul wrote that to the Romans.

Thomas: Oh.

Monk: And to us! Especially the so-called educated. Chesterton was brilliant. "Without education, we are in a horrible and deadly danger of taking educated people seriously!"

Thomas: You're telling me! But where do we go from here?

Monk: The truth has to assert itself. It has to have a voice in every generation. That's what sacred tradition is. This culture tells kids they're not allowed to question certain things… They're considered evil if they do. They're racist or homophobic or… old-fashioned! Outdated! As if new somehow means right! As if an opinion uttered on a Wednesday is more correct than one uttered on Tuesday!

Thomas: Am I supposed to help this young woman think through this at all?

Monk: Yeah!

Thomas: Well she's not thinking through it. She's not questioning.

Monk: Right, but you did it with your daughter. "Can you be an elephant?" "Why not?" God didn't make you an elephant. Who gave you your identity? The only one who can give you an identity is the one who made you. You can't self-identify as something else. Who made you? God made you! Why did God make you? To know, love, and serve Him in this life and be happy with Him forever in the next! Thomas, the desire for God is written on the human heart! But – and this is a big but – we go looking to fill that desire in some of the craziest places. I think that's why Jesus' first words in John's Gospel are so powerful. He's not only asking us but teaching us to ask others, "What are you looking for?"

Thomas: So we should do the same? Help people think about what they're really looking for?

Monk: Absolutely. Follow Him! He asks and so should we.
Thomas: And His questions are often rather uncomfortable.
Monk: Indeed.
Thomas: Sin… you said there are 3 requirements: It's against the will of God, you know it's against the will of God, and…
Monk: And you decide to do it.
Thomas: Let's say a kid tells me that he's thinking about some sin, for example premarital sex. If he doesn't know that it's wrong…
Monk: If the kid doesn't know that it's wrong, that's your fault. The sentence should not be out of his mouth before you…
Thomas: Even if I don't really know the person that well?
Monk: That's right. Because it's objective law, Thomas. It's not a sin because he thinks it's a sin. It's a sin because of the first premise of sin. It is taught by God as a sin.
Thomas: But if they don't know that, or if they don't believe that…
Monk: If they don't know that, then as I said, the sentence shouldn't even be out of their mouth before you correct it. You say, "That is a mortal sin, by the law of God, by the objective law of God." Whatever the right verbiage is for the situation. There is a difference between telling people the truth and leading people to the truth, yes?
Thomas: Definitely. That makes it personal responsibility. Then I'm responsible.
Monk: Exactly.
Thomas: They also have personal responsibility, but maybe not as much because they don't know it.
Monk: Again, Thomas, if they still don't know it…
Thomas: Well, let's say that I don't know them and they don't know that it's a sin?
Monk: Then what is your interaction, what is your responsibility?
Thomas: No interaction. I don't know them at all.
Monk: Then you have no responsibility.
Thomas: Right, but do they?
Monk: Of course they still have responsibility!

Thomas: But they don't know that it's wrong.
Monk: If they don't know that it's wrong, then, that's our fault. Any consent that they make to the act is an uninformed consent and, therefore, it's questionable whether or not the person is culpable.
Thomas: That makes sense.
Monk: You cannot sin if you don't know it's a sin. Now, if you don't *believe* it's a sin, even though you know the Church teaches against it, that's a whole different story! They guy who fails in his job as a sheepdog, okay, is cast out as a hireling. Jesus says so.
Thomas: So the teachers… Nicodemus – I remember reading this – Nicodemus went to Jesus and Jesus told him something to the tune of, "You consider yourself a teacher and you don't know this?"
Monk: Hmmm. And parents are teachers, yes?
Thomas: Yeah. Jesus kind of smacks him in the back of the head.
Monk: He said that to more people that Nicodemus.
Thomas: It seems like we've forgotten that. Jesus wasn't always – nice isn't the right word, but…
Monk: Oh, no! Ohhhhhh, no!
Thomas: He wasn't always kind. Was He always loving? I guess He was always loving, but brutal, sometimes brutal?
Monk: He was always Christ. Loving when you needed to be loved.
Thomas: And we're supposed to imitate that part of Him, too, I guess?
Monk: Well, yeah. That's sort of like His hands.
Thomas: That means if I'm not telling people the stuff they need to know or need to hear, I'm sinning, essentially.
Monk: Well, yeah, but, if they're not asking, alright?
Thomas: But you said earlier that you have to try to figure out what they're asking.
Monk: That's right!
Thomas: Even when they're not clear. Because they're not always asking stuff. Or when I get an obnoxious kid in confirmation class,

every now and then. They might be asking a different question and I have to figure it out.

Monk: Umm. The answer that you give them has to be…

Thomas: Correct. Ha!

Monk: …an open door to the Spirit. The answer that you give them is not, "Do this." Okay? The answer is, "This is what you've just said to me. Just take a couple minutes and think about what you're really asking here. Are you asking for permission to do something that you would rather do? Something that you know God doesn't want you to do? And, if that's the case, then what's the purpose? Is it selfishness? And if it is, why do you think you're inviting God into your life if you're telling Him that what He wants to make real and whole and wonderful in you… you're not interested.

Thomas: You have a different plan.

Monk: Disagreeing with God? "But Brother, I don't think that's a sin?" I'm sorry, these are not options. Not if you want to be a Catholic. You want to go to the "Church of What's Happening Now", well, then, go ahead. Form your own church. They can sing hymns to each other in Hell.

Thomas: Haha! John Wooden – the incredibly successful UCLA coach – called parenting the most important profession in the world!

Monk: And that's why I say get on your knees and pray about it!

Thomas: Pretty important!

Monk: Thomas, the decisions you make affecting your children are not less important to God than decisions the Pope makes regarding the Church. Your responsibility is not proportional. It's direct. God is not going to ask me generically. He's going to say, here's how you affected Thomas' spirituality. Just as He's going to say to you, here's what did for your wife. Here's what you did for your daughters. Here's how you impacted your Godson's faith.

Thomas: It's not big or little to God!

Monk: Right.

Thomas: It's always infinitely important, I guess?

Monk: Absolutely. Because it's interaction. You can't interact with another human being as a human being except that God gives you the voice, the intelligence, the… Not a sparrow falls from Heaven without His knowledge. You're worth much more than many sparrows, Jesus says. The analogy is very very clear. If the sparrow is important to God, and its individual falling from the sky. Is God conscious of all the birds falling from the sky – that's not the point. The point is, God's direct relationship with that which lives, with what He created… He never deals with us as a mob.

Thomas: So that would mean that the big things are individual big things, not mob big things?

Monk: You see, Thomas, we gave ourselves a hiding place. We call ourselves the people of God. Well, yeah, we're the holy people of God because we're the individual sons and daughters of God. We are guilty of this great global sin, but I'm not guilty of coveting my neighbor's wife. Because we made sin communal, it's corporate. No!

Thomas: So it's personal. And even the little things matter.

Monk: Again, Thomas, little in whose eyes? Not God's! Recall Catherine of Siena. Your soul is eternal! Matters more than a nation! That's a big deal.

Thomas: That's tough. A big job!

Monk: Yes. And it's yours. To whom much is given, much is required. Thomas, God made you a dad. A job you can't delegate.

Thomas: I'm blessed.

Monk: Yes, you are. More than you know. If we're going to engage people – friends, family, neighbors, our children – we've got to engage people in ways that they're going to sit still and listen, or sit still and watch, or sit still and ponder. That's not with a chalkboard any more. Of course, solid theological underpinning is of upmost importance. Of course the greatest stage, of course, is the Sanctuary. That's where the drama plays out. But they gotta know what's going on. It's like watching the 3rd Godfather without knowing what the series is all about. What happened to Michael Corleone? Trying to go legit, losing his favorite child. It was masterful. But if you don't know what it's all about, you're thinking, "Nice music, nice scenes, but so what?" It's the same with the Eucharist and the Liturgy. Father John Bertolucci used to say that if you had one inkling of what the Eucharist is, you'd crawl up on your hands and knees, weeping all the way. Of course that requires a whole revolution in thought as to what everything means. It's not just a check off all the boxes. Seriously, Thomas, why should we bother? Why go through all the trouble? Why put in the energy and effort to teach a confirmation class that truly engages? To connect this week's Gospel with something your neighbor is struggling with? To discuss a verse or the words of a saint with your spouse or kids? Why should a parent bother? Why should your pastor bother? Why should a religious ed teacher bother? Why bother? I try something like this… I'll get fired. Or the neighbors might think… Or my in-laws… Or my kids… Why stick my neck out? Who's expecting this? [long pause] *Except God!*

Thomas, I gotta go pray my midday office. Excuse me.

Thomas: How are you doing, Brother? You look tired. Why don't you take a nap after your midday office.

Monk: Yes.

19. Can I Lie for a Good Cause?

Thomas: What if I have a good reason to do the wrong thing?
Monk: Uh oh!
Thomas: But Brother, what if the ends justify the means?
Monk: Of course they do not.
Thomas: I should never do wrong…?
Monk: Never!
Thomas: … even if I think it's for a greater good?
Monk: It's one of the first principles of Scholastic Theology. You may never employ evil means, even for a good end.
Thomas: Who came up with that? I guess God did.
Monk: Thomas Aquinas. Well, he's the one who codified it, but it was around since the Apostles. Ignatius of Antioch, I think was the first one. Second century.
Thomas: Martin Luther King liked to quote Plato. He quoted a lot.
Monk: Talented man!
Thomas: Very much so. He harped on the idea that "the ends can't justify the means."
Monk: Um Hmmm.
Thomas: A lot of people seem to say the opposite today.
Monk: Most modern philosophy is entirely the opposite.
Thomas: If I get what I want… Popularity, fame, seem to be almost instant credibility today. Fame. You can be famous or infamous – you can be very famous for doing something that's incredibly bad. But that fame… the Kardashians, there are millions of examples… You get in the spotlight often by doing something that people think, "Whoah! That's outrageous!" That fame turns into almost instant credibility. Dr. King harped against this. Using unjust means to accomplish just ends. What you're saying is that what King said is valid.
Monk: Absolutely. That's one of the first principles of Christian morality.

Thomas: Can I lie to protect someone? For example, one of my favorite saints is Maximillian Kolbe.
Monk: That's because you're married to a Polish woman.
Thomas: Funny! He sacrificed his life in Auschwitz. Traded places with a man condemned to die by starvation. He had been arrested for hiding Jews in his monastery when the Nazis invaded Poland.
Monk: Heroic virtue.
Thomas: So that qualifies him to be a saint then?
Monk: Hmm.
Thomas: He's in heaven?
Monk: Church says so.
Thomas: You and I don't get to decide?
Monk: That's for sure! Where are you going with this?
Thomas: Someone like Kolbe, should he lie to the Nazis?
Monk: Lie about what?
Thomas: When they asked if he had Jews hidden?
Monk: Should he lie? No. Just say nothing. It's like confession.
Thomas: So, don't answer?
Monk: Because that is how you protect the truth. *Tacire non consentire*…To be silent is to protect. And not to consent.
Thomas: Okay. So I shouldn't lie. No matter what?
Monk: No, no! I'm not saying that. You asked me a specific question. "Should he have lied to save the Jews?" Okay?
Thomas: And you say no?
Monk: I'm saying no because he should have said nothing. That's how a priest protects the truth.
Thomas: Oh.
Monk: Now, there's the principle of double effect, which is the overriding principle of all ethics, medical ethics and other. What is the greater good to be accomplished and the greater evil to be avoided?
Thomas: That's called the law of double consequences?

Monk: *Principle* of Double *Effect!* Consequences get you in trouble. That's heresy. That's Consequentialism.
Thomas: Very different! Got it. Principle of Double Effect.
Monk: You cannot base a decision to act based on the consequences. It must be on the principle of a priori, value of the…
Thomas: Okay.
Monk: Okay. Here's the example. We Catholics are – well, at least the Catholic Church, fewer and fewer Catholics – are adamantly against abortion in any form. Supporting it. Voting for somebody who supports it, counseling someone to have it, by not preventing somebody from doing it… The Church teaches 9 ways you can participate in another person's sin.
Thomas: Wait!!! I can participate in… I can have guilt for… another person's sin?
Monk: Exactly. This is not new. There are 9 ways you can participate in another person's sin: 1. By counsel (to give advice) 2. By command (to demand or order) 3. By consent (to give permission, to approve, to agree to.) 4. By provocation (to dare.) 5. By praise or flattery (to cheer, to applaud, to commend.) 6. By concealment (to hide the action, to cover-up.) 7. By partaking (to take part, to participate.) 8. By silence (by playing dumb, by remaining quiet.) 9. By defense of the ill done (to justify, to argue in favor).
Thomas: That's some list! So, if you know somebody that might have an abortion and you don't try to you convince them otherwise…
Monk: That's right!
Thomas: You're guilty?
Monk: You're guilty of the sin.
Thomas: Whew!
Monk: Right. Yeah.

Thomas: What if I know someone, a father whose daughter might have an abortion. If I don't talk to my friend, the father of the young woman considering abortion, then I'm in. I'm involved?

Monk: Yes.

Thomas: As long as I know…

Monk: It's called material cooperation.

Thomas: Yeah.

Monk: You could've said something and did not.

Thomas: Okay.

Monk: Now, here's the principle. We are absolutely against abortion. There's no way that you can do a direct abortion. Okay?

Thomas: Sure.

Monk: Understand something. When you start getting into this, you'll find theology on abortion going back to the beginning of the Church. A procured abortion was excommunicatory since the Didache of the Apostles, our first canon law, before John the Apostle was dead.

Thomas: It was written about in the 1st Century?

Monk: Oh yeah. As excommunicatory.

Thomas: Those writings are still available?

Monk: Of course. Yes, it's available in English and the original Greek. A woman comes to me. She's pregnant. She's got a septic uterus. If I go to treat this, the baby will die.

Thomas: Yeah.

Monk: What do I do?

Thomas: You know the baby will die?

Monk: Yes. He's 6 weeks old.

Thomas: You wait, until the baby is older?

Monk: She'll be dead by then. Septic uterus.

Thomas: You have to treat it.

Monk: Why?

Thomas: Could you try to deliver the baby first?

Monk: No.

Thomas: …the baby's not old enough to survive outside the womb.
Monk: Principle of Double Effect. You're going the right direction. "How do we deliver the baby first?" That's why the principle of double effect is so important. What is the greater good to be accomplished? What is the greater evil to be avoided? You cannot do nothing. Christian charity says you've got to try to help this woman. God knows the state of our medical art, okay?
Thomas: Yeah.
Monk: You go in. If your intention is to abort the baby, you are morally completely equivocated. Your intention is to save this woman from death… In any case, if you don't treat it, the baby's going to die anyway with a septic uterus. But that's not the consideration. The consideration is, "What is your aim?" Your aim is to save her life because that's what Christ wants you to do.
Thomas: The greater good is the mother's life, then?
Monk: No. The greater good is doing what you have to do to save a life.
Thomas: A life.
Monk: Right.
Thomas: Either one?
Monk: But in this case you don't have a choice, with a 6-week-old baby. If, in the process of doing the good, an unintended evil occurs…
Thomas: But knowable! It's a knowable evil.
Monk: It is knowable, but not preventable… if you're going to save a life. It's unintended consequences. Okay? Then it is permissible to treat the septic uterus. Because you are not intending to harm the baby. The baby will die. God knows that. Your motive always matters, Thomas. And God knows your motive. That's why we so often hear the phrase "Judge not." …but we hear it used incorrectly. You hear people say, "Don't judge!" But we must judge actions, not motives. Unless we know the motive. If the doctor or mother says, "Let's abort the baby," the motive is clear. The difference is night

and day: know that the baby will die from a procedure versus intentionally killing that baby.

Thomas: So we go back to lying to save a life. You can do it if… you said you're supposed to not say anything, but you can do it if necessary. Part of the reason I bring this up is that kids absolutely, my kids, and I think adults, too, whether it's direct or indirect, are taught that there's no such thing as "This is the way you should behave." It's "You should behave this way, except under lots of… There's lots of…"

Monk: Caveats. Yeah.

Thomas: Right. And once there's one exception, it's easy for me to think, "Well, there's a second one and a third…

Monk: Dulls the conscience. Yeah.

Thomas: Or justification. What'd you call it?

Monk: Dulls the conscience. Repeated…

Thomas: Right. Here's a question they get in ethics classes: If a married woman is stranded on an island and the only off the island is to sleep with the guy that has the boat, the rescuer. What should she do you do?

Monk: What is the alternative?

Thomas: She dies on the island.

Monk: Right. Your obligation according to the 5th commandment is to preserve life, including your own.

Thomas: Then she should?

Monk: She has to save her life.

Thomas: Yeah.

Monk: That scumbag rescuer is committing the sin, if he's forcing her to do it. It's just like suicide is forbidden. You go straight to Hell. It's a sin against the Holy Spirit. If someone says that unless you put a bullet in your head, I'm going to put a bullet in your kids head, who's responsible for that suicide? That guy. Not you.

Thomas: That opens up the "there's a time when it's okay to do wrong…"

Monk: What is the greater good to be accomplished? What would be accomplished if she goes back faithful to her husband and she's dead, in a box?

Thomas: Okay. But do we know this stuff?

Monk: What do you mean, "do we know this stuff?"

Thomas: Well, I mean, you think through something like this and realize, "Wow, the right decision is blank." But there are so many decisions like this that people make…

Monk: That's why we need the Church. That's why we have Sacred Tradition, which is the living experience of Jesus Christ in every age. Christ didn't address nuclear war.

Thomas: And that should help answer these questions.

Monk: It doesn't *help*! It *answers* the questions. You've got to submit to the Truth of God. In other words, making these decisions that you agonize over… Look at Solomon. His decision to cut the baby in half. Did he ever intend to cut the baby in half? Probably! Because the king had that right, of life and death over every one of his subjects. But by saying that, he forced the principle of double effect. "No, give the baby to her. I'd much rather not even have my baby, as long as it can live." What's the greater good to be accomplished? Even though she would mourn that for the rest of her life, not having her baby.

Thomas: Wow. Of course. But it would still be alive. And she'd still see it.

Monk: Maybe she wouldn't.

Thomas: That's true.

Monk: Imagine if she couldn't even go over and touch her own child, nurse her own child, if she saw them in the crowd.

Thomas: So, are the ten commandments in order, then? Because you're saying I can lie, or I can commit adultery, if it's done to preserve a life.

Monk: That's not committing adultery.

Thomas: You're being forced.

Monk: Right. There is no sin where there is no consent, Thomas. Okay?
Thomas: But the consent would happen?
Monk: The consent has to be based on principles, other than your head.
Thomas: It's not really consent?
Monk: Otherwise, it's called heroic virtue. That's why people would rather be eaten by lions than denounce Christ. That's sainthood. You're not required heroic virtue.
Thomas: Okay. So, then the ten commandments are in order, to a degree?
Monk: In order of precedence? The first four deal with obligations to God, the next six deal with obligations to other people. But they're pretty much interchangeable. Like Saint Francis says, "He who offends against one offends against all."
Thomas: So, it takes a massive amount of… not a massive amount, but it takes a very clear justification – that might be the wrong word – reasoning… in order to do…
Monk: It takes a very clear assessment of…
Thomas: … things you know you shouldn't do, but…
Monk: Things that you should not do under normal circumstances. Thomas! There are three things necessary to commit a sin. It has to be objectively a sin by God's law. You have to know that it's objectively a sin by God's law. One and two are not operative unless number three kicks in, and that is, you have to totally consent to it.
Thomas: Oh.
Monk: Okay. Yes, you can commit a sin out of weakness, where you half consent and you half don't. But that's still in some sense… Father Cyril used to put this so beautifully, when I was asking him about hearing confessions, and how to make judgements. He said, "You gotta keep in mind, first of all, that there are sinners on both sides of the screen in the confessional. You have to keep that in

mind. The only priest who can be a good confessor is one remembers that he's been forgiven much. That's number 1.

Thomas: So, a lot of priests are probably not good confessors?

Monk: No. No one goes to confession anyways, so it's a moot point.

Thomas: True. Do you think that's part of the reason that people don't go?

Monk: Of course!

Thomas: They recently installed a statue of Padre Pio by one of the churches near my house. I love to go sit by that statue. It's outside and it's just a tiny statue, but I love to go there and think, "What are the things I wouldn't want to tell him?" You probably know his story. He would stop people mid-confession and say, "Come on! You're not telling me the whole story here."

Monk: Right. That's been my experience, too. I don't know where it comes from. I never met this person before.

Thomas: Don't you think that affects people going to confession? If you had a priest that did that, wouldn't you go more?

Monk: If you had a priest who asked tough questions, would you go more? Most people wouldn't. Because they have no idea what confession is for. They think it's for the forgiveness of their sins. That happened on the cross. It's an examination of conscience. That's why the Baltimore Catechism asks, "What is the first commandment?" Sin… trying to control what God has sovereignty over. When you go down the wrong path, you take your family, and your spirituality with you. People love to tell me that this idea of not living together before marriage is old-fashioned. 70% of marriages that result from people who were living together before marriage result in divorce. Old-fashioned! That is the Law of God from the time of the Apostles to this moment.

Thomas: "Old fashioned." "Outdated." "Back then." "They didn't know any better." You don't like these phrases so much?

Monk: Jesus Christ is the same, yesterday, today, and tomorrow.

20. Forgive Everyone? Seriously?

"All the darkness in the world cannot extinguish the light of a single candle." ~ St. Francis Of Assisi

Thomas: Am I just supposed to forgive everybody? For everything? No matter what?
Monk: Yes. Saint Paul runs through a whole list of people who are excluded from the Kingdom. Neither drunkards, nor adulterers…
Thomas: No one's getting in…
Monk: Nor thieves, nor liars, nor...
Thomas: It's like in the Sermon on the Mount when Jesus says… Lust. You've heard it said… don't commit adultery, but I say if you look at a woman with lust…
Monk: How do you interpret that? What is Jesus saying there?
Thomas: Hmmm. If you look at someone else and start thinking, "What kind of relationship could we have… What kind of things could we do together… What kind of pleasure can I get with that?" I guess that's how I look at it. Not to just see a woman and think, "Wow! She's beautiful." But to see someone and to think through adulterous acts without physically doing anything. That's my translation.
Monk: Uh Huh.
Thomas: Is that close?
Monk: Right, well, I'm asking what is Jesus' reaction to it. What is He saying to you about this? This is what you think He's saying? Defining. What is His reaction to it?
Thomas: His reaction to it?
Monk: He says, "If you look at a woman with lust, you've already committed adultery with her in your heart." What is He saying there?
Thomas: Big picture, I think He's saying no one is perfect.
Monk: Hmmm.

Thomas: You cannot earn your way into heaven. I think a lot of the Sermon on the Mount is… The bar is higher than you ever thought and you can't get there without help. In the Sermon on the Mount, wasn't He talking to everybody? Didn't he likely share those messages repeatedly?
Monk: Ah, yes, but the ones who used to get closest to Him, to fight with Him, were the scribes and the pharisees… They put themselves right there, at His feet, so they could shout Him down and argue with Him in front of the people.
Thomas: Okay. And?
Monk: The pharisees… the story of the adulterous woman… the pharisees stand as the great condemners.
Thomas: Yes.
Monk: And Jesus makes a very clear point with the pharisees. What you think righteousness is will never get you anywhere near the Kingdom of Heaven. And so, in addition to saying that the action is the child of the thought or the desire, He's also saying to them, "You're using this to condemn others, while you are just as guilty and, therefore, your condemnatory power is hereby cancelled." In other words, you condemn this person? Hypocrite!
Thomas: You've done the same thing! In a different way.
Monk: At least in your thoughts. Look at the situation of the woman caught in adultery. The Law of Moses says people caught in adultery, both the man and the woman, have to be stoned. So they drag this woman in front of Jesus and say we caught her in adultery. If you *caught* her in adultery, what does that mean?
Thomas: Where's the other person? Where's the guy?
Monk: Aha! Ahhhh!
Thomas: Maybe he's one of them? Or not one of them, but one of their friends or supporters?
Monk: No. If he was a Jew, he would be there.
Thomas: Oh.

Monk: They both have to be condemned if they're caught in adultery, according to the Law of Moses. See? So where is he? This woman was caught in adultery. Which means you came upon two people. One of whom you could seize and one of whom you couldn't.

Thomas: One was Roman? Maybe?

Monk: Well, he wasn't a Jew. So, when Jesus bends down and writes on the ground in response to their question, Jesus knows. Her husband is disabled or her husband has been killed. She has a Roman soldier who will feed her kids if she sleeps with him.

Thomas: Oh wow.

Monk: Husband's not dead because she's in adultery. And that's what I believe and what Saint Cyril believed was what Jesus was writing on the ground. This woman has not committed adultery. She had no consent. She had to feed her kids. Principle of double effect.

Thomas: He was writing the other side of the story, or the back story.

Monk: And that's why He stands up and says, "Let you who is without sin cast the first stone." How can you judge this woman? You don't know anything about her. You have no idea what I know about her.

Thomas: Yeah.

Monk: And again, that puts it into the perspective of this external act of adultery or whatever the sin may be.

Thomas: He's saying don't judge her. But He's saying don't judge her whole being, right? Judging her actions is different.

Monk: No. We can't judge her because you don't know what the action is.

Thomas: You don't know the motive behind the action.

Monk: The whole point is that she's not committed adultery because she didn't consent. They're making the judgement that she did commit adultery. According to the objective criteria for adultery, she slept with a man who was not her husband. That is objectively disordered. But, if you don't consent to it, you are not part of the disorder. What is the greater good to be accomplished? Should she let her kids starve?

Thomas: We don't know that. He knows that, I guess. But do they know that?

Monk: Who are you talking about?

Thomas: Do the people that want her stoned, do they know that?

Monk: That's the whole point. They don't know it and so they can't condemn!

Thomas: Can you condemn anyone, then?

Monk: No! He says so. "Condemn not and ye shall not be condemned."

Thomas: Even a murderer? A murderer! Do you condemn a murderer?

Monk: No. You don't condemn anyone. A murderer is condemned by his own action. In other words, it's not an objective law. God does not punish. The murderer has, whether he admits it or not, has brought anti-life into his own existence by his actions.

Thomas: Okay.

Monk: Now, society's idea of justice, that's a whole different discussion. The Christian has to forgive the murderer. Society… it's always been taught that society has to protect itself and that leads to justice and prison and capital punishment.

Thomas: If you're not a biblical scholar, how would you know some of these things? How would the normal person know these things? I mean, somebody in the "real world", am I supposed to just forgive anyone that ever does anything bad to me? For example, in business relationships, should I trust someone if they've consistently shown themselves to not be trustworthy? Should I forgive them, but not work with them anymore? How does someone live this in the practical world?

Monk: I quote Saint Ronald Reagan.

Thomas: Ha! Saint Ronald Reagan!

Monk: Trust, but verify.

Thomas: *Doveryai no proveryai.* Yes! He said it in Russian a lot. Trust, but verify.

Monk: Heheheh!

Thomas: So, you can do that, but you're not judging them because you don't know them. You don't know their back story.

Monk: To be wary is not judging someone.

Thomas: It's being a good steward. Of life, of resources, of your time.

Monk: But forgiving them… You must. You must! To trust them again, that's not part of the requirement.

Thomas: I don't forgive everyone perfectly.

Monk: Ahhh! Then your heavenly Father will not forgive you.

Thomas: Do you? Come on, who really forgives everyone perfectly? Doesn't that go with none of us can earn our way in?

Monk: That's an important insight about earning your way in and not forgiving everyone. But, see, forgiving is an act of the will. Not forgiving is also an act of the will.

Thomas: Yes.

Monk: You see? So it's not a matter of "I just can't forgive this person because of my feelings." You're not required to have good feelings about people.

Thomas: To feel good towards them.

Monk: By making a conscious decision to … by forgiveness, we mean Christian forgiveness, not putting them on probation. Not saying, "you got away with it this time, but if you do it again…"

Thomas: Right.

Monk: If my brother sins against me 70 times, do I forgive him? Yes, 70 times 7 times.

Thomas: But it goes back to that trust but verify. It doesn't mean you let them watch your kids again, or lend them money again, or employ them to manage your business…

Monk: You can have a slice of my bread, but you can't have my daughter…

Thomas: Love people. Forgive people. Sounds so perfect, until you interact with some of those special people. I used to say that I liked people. But some people will walk all over you. Give 'em an inch and they'll take a mile!

Monk: Did not the Son of Man have to undergo all these things so as to enter into His glory?

Thomas: Brother, do you remember my bus business? One of my employees stole the whole business. That was a tough one to forgive. I usually joke when I tell the story. I thought almost the exact opposite of what Jesus said. I thought, "Don't forgive him because he knew exactly what he was doing." He knew what he was doing. He knew exactly what he was doing. I guess maybe the back story… But my job is to forgive him, regardless of the back story?

Monk: Thomas! Do you want God to only forgive you when you don't know what you're doing?

Thomas: No.

Monk: The reason you need forgiveness is because you knew precisely what you were doing. That's why it's a sin.

Thomas: Of course.

Monk: And so your Heavenly Father will treat you.

Thomas: Well, I was mad as you could imagine at the guy for a while.

Monk: I only heard snippets of that story. He stole the business?

Thomas: He was my right hand guy. We taught him everything about the business. And he was going to buy the whole business. And then, we're going through everything so that he can run the whole business. After months of this, he says, "I don't think I'm going to buy the business any more." He started systematically stealing all of our customers… telling them that we were re-branding and signing contracts with them under the new name. At the same time, we started having every imaginable mechanical problem. Almost as if none of the routine maintenance was being done on any of our vehicles.

Monk: Where'd you find this guy?

Thomas: He was one of my employees. He was actually one of the best employees we ever had.

Monk: Then Satan entered his heart. The whole debacle here, even though it's represented here in money and business… The sin is the way he treated you. Sin has to be interpersonal. You can't sin against the cattle industry.

Thomas: But a group of people you could, couldn't you?

Monk: What do you mean?

Thomas: When somebody bombs an embassy because they hate the United States. They decide that they hate a country, the U.S., that's not personal.

Monk: Well, it is personal. They've decided that this person hates those persons. And the harm is done to the person, not the brick and windows of the embassy. Or, in your case, the harm is done to you, not the business. Recall the prodigal son story… The prodigal son returns and says to the Father, "I have sinned against you and against God." This man who stole your business – he sinned against you and against God.

Thomas: And I should forgive him?

Monk: We pray it all the time. Forgive us our trespasses… as we forgive those who trespass against us. Forgive me the way I forgive that neighbor, in-law, former boss, the guy cut me off in traffic or the one who stole my business. Father, forgive me the way I forgive! As you forgive those who sin against you so will your Heavenly Father will also forgive you!

21. Let Him Love You!

The is but a small sampling from over a decade of conversations with the Monk. But it's not over. My hope is that this is just a beginning. One of the greatest gifts the Monk gave me: the chance to wrestle with life's most important questions. He welcomed questions. Inspired questions. Pursued questions.

I was blessed to spend many hours with him in the last year of his life as he battled a very aggressive cancer. We recorded hours of conversations in an effort to make this book as true to his incredible conversations as possible. Brother asked me to share some of those audio clips with you. Some challenging, inspiring, and thought-provoking clips: www.JonathanFanning.com/monk.

I was deeply saddened when the Monk passed away. He was a gift. A priceless gift. I miss him. I think he would tell us this:

We are not meant to walk alone. You have monks in your life. Closer than you think. You may have to go looking for them, give them a little more of your time, or initiate more meaningful conversations with them. And you are called to be a Monk for someone. That doesn't mean you have all the answers. As Brother so often reminded me, you and I get to be sheepdogs. Our job is to point towards the Shepherd. Point towards Truth. Point towards Goodness. Point towards Beauty. Point towards God. Help people God puts in your life to figure out what they are looking for. And help them seek true answers to their God-given quest!

Ask the Monk to pray for you and with you. But watch out! Brother often told me that the saints would certainly see our challenges differently than we do. As a result, their prayers might be a lot more closely aligned with the wildness of God. Let God invite you on an adventure that you can't even imagine. Do you think God wants to play a bigger role in your life? Will you let Him?

And let God love you through it all. Let Him love you.

About the Author

Jonathan Fanning is the author of several books, including ***Who are you BECOMING?***, ***Creativity Unleashed*** and ***I Once Was Lost***. He has inspired and challenged audiences with his message in 49 states and on 3 continents. Jonathan was voted the best speaker at a TEDx conference. He speaks for companies, non-profits, schools, parenting groups, and churches. A traumatic car accident and several other "Frying Pan" moments in the middle of Fanning's career as a management consultant provided a much needed wake-up call. *"Who are you BECOMING?"* and *"Who are you helping the people around you to BECOME?"* became central to Jonathan's life, business, and speaking. He has built and operated several successful businesses, including a national children's fitness franchise and Entrepreneur Adventure, designed to help young people experience business start-up and ownership. Jonathan lives in NY with his amazing wife and two precious daughters.

Keynotes, workshops, retreats and coaching programs include:

- *Who are you BECOMING?*
- *Set the World on Fire (Church Retreat or Talk)*
- *The Servant Leader Paradox: Leaders we Choose to Follow*
- *Creativity Unleashed: 5 Habits of World-Class Innovators*
- *Developing Emotional Intelligence*
- *Conversations with the Monk*

For more information, engaging videos, and thought-provoking content that compliments this book, visit us online:

www.JonathanFanning.com

Made in the USA
Middletown, DE
07 February 2025

70328952R00104